DEPTH PERCEPTION

ALSO BY ROBIN MORGAN

POETRY

Monster

Lady of the Beasts

NONFICTION

Going Too Far: The Personal Chronicle of a Feminist

ANTHOLOGIES

Sisterhood Is Powerful (ed.)

The New Woman (ed.)

ROBIN MORGAN

Depth Perception

NEW POEMS AND A MASQUE

ANCHOR BOOKS
Anchor Press/Doubleday
Garden City, New York
1982

The author gratefully acknowledges that work on some of the following poems was aided by the award of a National Endowment for the Arts Literature Grant in Poetry, for the year 1979–1980. Furthermore, the author wishes to express appreciation to the artists' colony Yaddo; some of these poems were written while an artist-in-residence there in spring, 1980.

Some of these poems appeared earlier in *Feminist Studies, Kalliope, Maenad, Sojourner, The Second Wave, 13th Moon,* and *Woman/Poet.*

"Nature's Garden: An Aid to the Knowledge of Wild Flowers," first appeared in Calyx, a Journal of Art and Literature by Women, Volume 5 #1, June 1980.

"The Ruining of the Work" was first published in *New England Review,* together with its complementary poem, "The Uniting of the Opposites" by Kenneth Pitchford; the two works appeared as halves of a joint poem titled, in its entirety, "The Ruining and the Uniting."

"The Fall of a Sparrow" first appeared in *The American Poetry Review.*

Ms. Magazine originally published the poems "Battery," "Peony," and "Aerial View," as well as an earlier, excerpted version of "The Duel: A Masque."

"The Duel: A Masque in One Act" had its performance debut on May 7, 1979, at Joseph Papp's New York Shakespeare Festival Public Theater, together with Kenneth Pitchford's complementary one-act play, "The Dialectic." The two works, together entitled *Love's Duel,* were directed by Gilda Grillo, and were a production of the Poets at the Public Series.

Some of these poems appeared as a limited-edition chapbook, *Death Benefits,* published by Copper Canyon Press (Port Townsend, Washington, 1981).

All rights to "The Duel: A Masque," including professional, amateur, motion picture, recitation, lecturing, public reading, radio broadcasting, television, and the rights of translation into foreign languages, are strictly reserved. All inquiries concerning these rights should be addressed to the author's representative, Edite Kroll, 31 East 31st Street, New York, NY 10016.

Excerpt from *A Passage to India* by E. M. Forster © 1924 by Harcourt Brace Jovanovich Inc.; renewed in 1952 by E. M. Forster. Reprinted by permission of the publisher.

Excerpt from "An Ordinary Evening in New Haven" from *The Collected Poems of Wallace Stevens* © 1950 by Wallace Stevens. Reprinted by permission of Alfred A. Knopf, Inc.

Excerpts from *Poems of Akhmatova,* selected, translated, and introduced by Stanley Kunitz with Max Hayward copyright © 1973 by Stanley Kunitz and Max Hayward. First appeared in *Poetry.* By permission of Little, Brown and Company in association with the Atlantic Monthly Press.

Depth Perception is published simultaneously in hardcover and paperback editions.

Library of Congress Cataloging in Publication Data
Morgan, Robin.
  Depth perception.
  I. Title.
PS3563.O87148D4   811'.54
AACR2
ISBN 0-385-17794-1
ISBN 0-385-17795-X (pbk.)
Library of Congress Catalog Card Number 81–47868

CONTENTS

"Apri gli occhi e riguarda qual son io."
"Il Paradiso" (xxiii, 46),
Dante's *Commedia*

DEPTH PERCEPTION

ONE

PIECING

(for Lois Sasson)

> "Sometimes you don't have no control over the way things are. Hail ruins the crops, or fire burns you out. And then you're just given so much to work with in a life and you have to do the best you can with what you got. That's what piecing is. The materials is passed on to you, or is all you can afford. But the way you put them together is your business. You can put them in any order you like. Piecing is orderly."
>
> An anonymous woman quoted
> in *The Quilters: Women and
> Domestic Art*

Frugality is not the point. Nor waste.
It's just that very little is discarded
in any honest spending of the self,
and what remains is used and used
again, worn thin by use, softened
to the pliancy and the translucence
of old linen, patched, mended, reinforced,
and saved. So I discover how
I am rejoicing slowly into a woman
who grows older daring to write
the same poem over and over, not merely
rearranged, revised, reworded, but one poem
hundreds of times anew.

The gaudy anniversaries.
The strips of colorless days gone unexamined.
This piece of watered silk almost as shot with light
as a glance he gave me once. This sturdy
canvas shred of humor. That fragment of pearl velvet,
a particular snowstorm. Assorted samples of anger—
in oilcloth, in taffeta, in tufted chenille,
in every imaginable synthetic and ready-to-wear.
This diamond of tie-dyed flannel baby-blanket;

that other texture of deception, its dimensional embroidery.
A segment of bleached muslin still crisp with indifference.
This torn veil of chiffon, pewter as the rain
we wept through one entire July. These brightly printed
squares across which different familiar figures
walk through parks or juggle intricate abstract designs.
Two butterflies of yellow organdy my mother cut
when I was eight months old. A mango gros-grain ribbon
fading off toward peach. The corner of an old batik
showing one small window that looked out on—what?
A series of simple cotton triangles in primary colors.
And this octagonal oddment: a sunburst or mandala or pinwheel
radiating rainbow stripes against what turns out
upon close inspection to be a densely flowered background.
It's striking enough to be a centerpiece.

Once I thought this work could be less solitary.
Many of us, I imagined, would range ourselves
along the edges of some pattern we would all agree on
well beforehand, talking quietly while we worked
each with her unique stitch inward to the same shared center.

This can still be done, of course, but some designs
emerge before they can be planned, much less agreed on,
demand an entire life's work, and are best viewed upon completion.
And then, so many designers bore too easily
to work the same theme over and over, with only
the slightest gradual adjustments, like subtly changing
your thread from brown to gray.

Still, the doorbell does toll in visitors, some of whom
slash rents across the section just perfected
        —all without meaning to,
and some of whom admire the audacity or quality
of scraps—but rarely notice the order, which is
the one thing you control. But some contribute:
a quarter yard of paisley, or a length of gauze
fine enough for bandages. Once somebody left behind

an entire pocket of gold lamé, all by itself.
The challenge is to use it so
that the tarnished griefs she stuffed it with
to lend it shape need be no longer hidden.

Throwing such a piece away is not the answer. Nor
has hoarding anything to do with this.
And nobody really hazards piecework in the expectation
that someday all these fragments might inevitably

                                        fit

into a gentle billow of warmth, to comfort
the longest winter sleep.
Not even that.
It's just the pleasure of rescuing some particle
into meaning. For a while.

Of course, this means that you yourself
are placed where you risk being
worn all the more severely
into translucent linen, held up
toward the light.

HEIRLOOM

For weeks now certain hours of every day
have been wiped sterile by the visit
to her hospital room where semi-privately
she semi-lives. For weeks
I've sourly reveled in the duty
while loathing its victim—my philanthropy
about as gracious as the bestowal of a poison cup
on a thirsty beggar who embodies a convenient excuse
but with a regrettable smell.

For days I've watched her reason fracturing
faster even than her body's fragmentation, as each
cell gradually detaches itself and shudders off
via the Parkinson method of interentropic travel.
For days the medication has made her more intense
than usual: cantankerous, weepy, domineering, sentimental,
and and and repetitive, a record that *will* not break
but always seems about to—the scratch on her soul itself.
No wonder she's abrasive. The wonder is,
since nothing will help her anyway,
that I can still be so ungenerous.

But then this afternoon we took each other
by surprise at the quite unexpected intersection
of Insanity and Humor—La Place de la Hallucination.
Forget that she frequently remembers I'm her sister,
or her mother, or her niece, or myself—her own child
but four years old again. Today she had some style.
Or something in me finally recognized whose style it was
I thought I'd made my own.

The patent-leather shoe with the round white buckle
had no business being up there on the night-table, even
if it did ring so insistently. The fly that walked the track
on which the room-partitioning curtain could be pulled

was going to get run over but he refused to listen to advice.
The teensy lady who perched cross-legged on the windowsill
while wearing the whole poinsettia plant right in her hat
really should have left much earlier—but people just don't
realize how visitors can tire a popular patient out.
And whoever had sent the basket of Florida newborn babies' heads
certainly had weird taste.

And I, who should know better, who at a younger age and chemistry
than she have heard radio static stutter in strict rhyme,
flinched from a Navaho blanket that snapped its teeth at me,
watched beloved faces leer with helpful malice—
I find myself explaining to her
What Is Really There. Except she's caught me
as suddenly as I catch her, and in astonishment
I shrug and say, "You seeing 'em again, huh? Well,
whatthehell, why not. What else is there to see?"

—and miracle of bitter miracle, she laughs.
And helpless I am laughing and the semi-roommate laughs
and the invisible lady in the poinsettia hat
can be heard distinctly laughing
and in this space of semi-dying there is life
and magic and shared paranoia thicker than water
and more clear than blood and we are laughing
while the bright shoe rings
and the fly dares death
and the oranges clamor to be fed
and all the thousand spear-carrying extras
direct from Central Casting come scurrying in
got up in white to hustle us apart—
as if our waving to each other weren't a sign
beyond their understanding;
as if the giggly last whisper, "Try to get through
the night any old way you can, Love. See you
in the morning," weren't a hiccuped message
encoded too deep in each of all our lonely cells
for any deciphering.

DEATH BENEFITS

What might I do to get beyond
living all these lives of quiet
courage too close for comfort
to endurance or mere suffering
or graceless martyrdom—all of which
equal cowardice: the unsaid, undone, unheard,
unthought of, and undreamt undoing of what
I've undeniably understood
this undertaking would unfold
or even (unconventionally) unify?

"Leave your loved ones
fixed for life," the saying goes—and stays.
Life insurance and death benefits
are what a sensible person hopes for.

Meanwhile, Denial
leaks from our containment vessels
and passes through the doors and walls
of houses, flats, lungs, conversations,
an odorless, tasteless, non-discriminating
equal opportunity destroyer,
the blinded head proud in its even,
ceaseless, swivel.

Is it Denial then I follow in a burst
of irritation with my own obsessive focus
on one subject: this man, this woman, their
tiresome and pretentiously embattled love?
Others are aging and dying, sharing a crisis
of energy, sickening, telling kind lies,
outgrowing commitments, not getting involved.
Others, long starved into hatred, are killing
still others for the death benefit that reassures

them they are not merely part of a tactical phase.
Others glide through back alleys, blunted
triangles of shadow, movable famines, bolts
of coarse cloth whispering How disrespectful
to god it would be to appear
out in public not wearing scar tissue.
Besides, it's protective, they add, turning
away. Why is that swivel familiar?

How can Denial deny coexisting
with the fiddlehead fern even as it exudes
its own Bach Air for Cello too loud
for our ears? Or, wordless, deny
how a cat celebrates its own tongue
with each suave coral yawn? Still,
before Affirmation becomes a denial
remember that this time cat, frond, and
melody too will be forced
to share benefits deadly as our own
denial of what they have never protested to be
their own innocence—too pure for that.

Which is not a disclaimer. I too have had policies,
kept up my payments, gone veiled, benefited
from death—and denial of death.
And thought of cashing it in, more than once,
really fixing my loved ones for life,
escaping now, here, eluding what's due to me
anyway on its maturity, swiveling once and for all
beyond any benefits I could accrue
through denial of what is denied to be life.

To deny that insurance, of course, breaks
the scar tissue open, leaking what we yet could
say, do, hear, think of, understand, dream
from the containment, leaking a different
radiance over bared heads.

What might I do then to get beyond
dying so many lives of affirming Denial?

Who is this figure I swivel behind like a shadow?
Who are the woman and man I'm being drawn back to—
again, the flaw here, the fall now, the original
schism, the atom entire?

Policies lapse. Nothing is sure
any longer. That fact alone is
a renegade benefit, something like grace,
green, mimetic, audacious—daring to bleed,
sing, embrace simply each other, to find
in those arms a planet entire, swiveling up
at us its azure, full face,
blinking new eyes, yawning into a loud
rain of relief to be home. Almost as if,
this late, unveiled and forgiven, even
Denial might weep again. And if not here,
where, you ask; if not now, when? Oh my dear,
who am I to deny?

NATURE'S GARDEN:
AN AID TO KNOWLEDGE OF WILD FLOWERS

The Wake-Robin, or Nodding Trillium, droops
three whitely margined petals under a whorl
of rhombic leaves. This is its season
in Eastern thickets, though it can thrive
westward to Missouri, south to Georgia.
In late summer an egg-shaped, pendulous berry
will poise at the summit, pealing color deep
as a ruby crystal.

Some say these roots are poisonous; in them
the next year's leaves lie curled throughout
the winter, as in the iris and Solomon's seal.
So do we bring our blizzard closeness safely
through the spring in cities, but under the same
May moon, a nightsky's unplucked, thickening eyebrow
wryly arched over our doorstep, where
a junkie, not a trillium, nods.

They have torn down that other building
where sixteen years ago this night
we first wound like the vines of Purple Virgin's Bower
around the steep and rocky elevations
of each other's naked love.
Leaves of wax saved from a candle
that blazed us through till dawn
still celebrate how the wick's spine dances
in this our ritual burning.

Leaves of poems still lie curled in our roots,
though as we age it grows more difficult
to separate who felt which thought
or merely spoke it first aloud.

He never brought me flowers in those years.
But one day bore me home, despite

our poverties of various kinds, a wilted book
found growing in the gutter, literally
discarded there until he plucked it up.
He always understood the ways of reclamation
better than those of purchase, fearing
merchants the way an archeologist might wince
to see fifty identical ancient wine-cups hawked
with hand-painted fervor at a bazaar.

But this was a bouquet. Such a bouquet!—
of Four-Leafed Laughing Loostrife,
Trout Lily, Mother's Heart (a small white flower
with notched pods, boat-shaped petals, and arrow
leaves clasping its stem, its distribution nearly
the entire earth). And Bunk. And Lizard's Tail,
and Devil's Paintbrush, and the double putty orchid
they call Adam and Eve, and hundreds more to bloom
and wither, seed and pollinate, creep, twine,
wilt, and root, in poem upon poem like a High Heal-All
of the wounds we gave one another,
like a Ghost-Flower of the courting we never did,
like the Fever-Bush of our lifelong battle
or the Scarlet Painted Cup from which
we drank our fatal potion—

this bouquet. And do you think that fifty
identical hothouse roses could compete?
Or do you understand the gift
of such a spring as this might not transform
even our city rubble, the miracle
unearthed over and over, rippling
as if through the focus of a ruby
its wick-brief incandescence, its citysunrise
ripeness, its carillon at matins singing
Wake-Robin! Wake-Robin!
—to discover it was not a dream?

PEONY

(for Suzanne Braun Levine)

What appears to be
this frozen explosion of petals
abristle with extremist beauty
like an entire bouquet on a single stem
or a full chorus creamy-robed rippling
to its feet for the *sanctus*—
is after all a flower,
perishable, with a peculiar
history. Each peony
blossoms only after
the waxy casing thick around
its tight green bud is eaten literally
away by certain small herbivorous ants
who swarm round the stubborn rind
and nibble gently for weeks to release
the implosion called a flower. If
the tiny coral-colored ants have been
destroyed, the bloom cannot unfist itself
no matter how carefully forced to umbrage
by the finest hothouse gardeners.

Unrecognized, how recognizable:

Each of us nibbling discreetly
to release the flower,
usually not even knowing
the purpose—only the hunger;

each mostly unaware of any others,
sometimes surprised by a neighbor,
sometimes (so rarely) astonished
by a glimpse into one corner
at how many of us there are;

enough to cling at least, swarm back,
remain, whenever we're shaken
off or drenched away
by the well-meaning gardener, ignorant
as we are of our mission, of our being
equal in and to the task.

Unequal to the task: a word
like "revolution," to describe
what our drudge-cheerful midwifery
will bring to bear—with us not here
to see it, satiated, long since
rinsed away, the job complete.

Why then do I feel this tremble,
more like a contraction's aftermath
release, relax, relief
than like an earthquake; more
like a rustling in the belly,
or the resonance a song might make
en route from brain to larynx—
      as if now, here, unleaving itself of all
      old and unnecessary outer layers

            butterfly from chrysalis
            snake from cast skin
            crustacean from shell
            baby from placenta

something alive before
only in Anywoman's dreamings
begins to stretch, arch, unfold
each vein on each transparency opening proud,
unique, unduplicate,
each petal stiff with tenderness,
each gauzy wing a different shading flecked
ivory silver tangerine moon cinnamon amber flame
hosannas of lucidity and love in a wild riot,

a confusion of boisterous order
all fragrance, laughter, tousled celebration—
     only a fading streak like blood
     at the center, to remind us we were there once

          but are still here, who dare, tenacious,
          to nibble toward such blossoming
          of this green stubborn bud
          some call a world.

TWO

THREE DEFINITIONS OF POETRY

1

Two thousand years ago, the Chinese
Princess Tou Wan designed herself
a burial suit which would preserve her
body for all time. This armor,
a mosaic of jade fragments tied
with pure gold thread, is still intact,
untarnished, the moss-blue veins still subtle
in contrast to the bright metallic arteries.
Within the shape of her own mold, Tou Wan
is safe as dust.

2

Birth is the mortal wound,
life the infection entering in.
Love is the fever, truth the chill.
Age forms the scab dying alone rips free.
Some pick at it every day
while others try to soften it
by soaking in salt-water. And some
do wrench it off with one swift motion.
Art lies in the x-ray, as you might have guessed—
the whole story in negative,
the diagnosis, treatment, relapses
and remissions. Unless this record is misfiled
or overexposed.

3

Outside it's raining catatonics and dogmatics.
Inside, inside the room, inside the cover
of the cage, inside the cage itself, inside the head

under the hunched wing, the eyes of the poem
tick, unblinking, in sockets of oil.
When the cage cover is removed, everyone marvels at
such spontaneity of song.

BATTERY

The fist meets the face as the stone meets water.
I want to understand the stone's parabola
and where the ripples disappear,
to make the connections, to trace
the withholding of love as the ultimate violence.

Battery: a word with seven letters, seven definitions:

1) Any unit, apparatus, or grouping
in which a series or set of parts or components
is assembled to serve a common end.
2) *Electrical.* One or more primary or secondary cells
operating together as a single source of direct current.
3) *Military.* A tactical artillery unit.
4) *A game position.* In baseball, the pitcher
and catcher together.
5) *Law.* The illegal beating or touching of another person.
6) *Music.* The percussion instruments of an orchestra.
7) *Optics.* The group of prisms in a spectroscope.

I want to understand the connections
—between the tower where Bertha Mason Rochester
is displayed to Jane Eyre as a warning
—with this place, this city, my doorstep
where I've learned to interfere between
the prostitute's scream and the pimp's knife
is to invite their unified disgust.

I want to understand the components:
—the stone's parabola, the percussion instruments,
the growth of battered children into battered wives
who beat their children,
—the beating of the fallow deer in Central Park Zoo
by unknown teenage assailants,
—the beating of these words against the poem:

to hit, slap, strike, punch, slash, stamp,
pound, maul, pummel, hammer, bludgeon, batter—
to hurt, to wound,
to flex the fist and clench the jaw and withhold love.

I want to discover the source of direct current,
to comprehend the way the primary or secondary cells
operate together as that source:
—the suburban community's defense of the fugitive Nazi
discovered to be a neighbor,
—the effect of her father's way with women
on the foreign policy of Elizabeth Tudor,
—the volunteers for a Utah firing squad,
the manner in which kwashiorkor—Red Johnny,
the Ghanaians call this slow death by starvation—
turns the hair of children a coppery color
with the texture of frayed wire.

I want to follow the refractions of the prism:
—the water's surface shuddering in anticipation
of the arching pebble,
—the oilslick mask imposed on the Pacific,
—the women of the Irish peace movement accused
of being traitors to tactical artillery units on both sides,
and replying, "We must accept that
in the next few months we will become their targets,"
—the battering of dolphins against tuna nets,
—the way celosia, a flower commonly known
as cockscomb, is bulbous, unpetaled, and a dark velvet red—
and always reminds me of a hemorrhaging brain.

The danger in making the connections
is to lose the focus,
and this is not a poem about official torture
in Iran or Chile or Poland, or a poem about
a bald eagle flailing its wings as it dies,
shot down over Long Island.
This is a poem called "Battery" about a specific woman
who is twelve-going-on-seventy-three and who

exists in any unit, grouping, class, to serve a common end.
A woman who is black and white and bruised all over
the world, and has no other place to go
—while the Rolling Stones demand shelter
—and some cops say it's her own fault for living with him
—and some feminists say it's her own fault for living with him,
and she hides her dark red velvet wounds
from pride, the pride of the victim,
the pride of the victim at not
being the perpetrator,
the pride of the victim at not knowing how
to withhold love.

The danger of fixing on the focus
is to lose the connections, and this is a poem
about the pitcher and the catcher *together*:
—the battery of Alice Toklas, conversing cookbooks
with the other wives while Gertrude Stein shared her cigars
and her ideas with the men,
—the sullen efficiency of Grace Poole,
—the percussion of my palm striking my husband's face
in fury when he won't learn how to fight back, how to outgrow
having been a battered child, his mother's battered wince
rippling from his eyes, his father's laborer's fingers
flexing my fist, the pitcher and the catcher together
teaching me how to withhold love;
the contempt of the perpetrator for the pride of the victim.
The collaboration, the responsibility, the intimate
violence, the fantasy, the psychic battery, the lies,
the beating of the heart.

To fear, to dread, to cower, cringe, flinch,
shudder—to skulk, to shuffle.

Wing-beat, heart-beat,
the fist meets the face as the stone displaces water,
as the elbow is dislocated from the socket
and the connections shatter from the focus;
—the knifeblade glimmers in the streetlight;

—it could be a drifting eagle feather
or cigar smoke rising
graceful as a doe who leaps in pain,
rising livid as a welt, livid as a consciousness
of my own hand falling to dispense
the bar of soap, the executioner's axe, the tuna nets,
the rifles, and at last the flint
for Bertha Mason Rochester to strike,
to spark the single source of direct current,
to orchestrate the common end emprismed
in the violent ripples of withheld love.

Batter my heart, seven-petaled word—for you
as yet but flower inside my brain—
that I may understand the stone's parabola,
make the connections, remember the focus,
comprehend the definitions,
and withhold nothing.

TWO BY TWO

Epithalamium
(*for K.L. and M.K.*)

This bride's bouquet of fragrant, touseled lives,
this revolution we take turns tossing to each other,
is bright with our diversity of loves,
a metaphor mixed with blood and laughter.
We are about love—wild and tame—the risks
of love-in-anger, love-in-fear, love-that-lets-go
and love-at-peace, love equal to the tasks
of cooking an omelette on a rainy Sunday,
changing the world, going to jail;
passion and embarrassment, committed. Easy, no. Possible, yes.
Dear, daring friends, I wish you well
from my own tightrope taut with two decades of this—
praising the love that moves the sun and other stars,
and moves her hand. And his. And mine. And yours.

Epitaph
(*for S.P. and E.M.*)

Always the waiting, the labor, the stillborn word;
never the cord cut clean, the cry, the light.
Always she whispered too loud to be heard,
never could he breathe freely of her doubt.
Always their faith that love was for the willing
(never their trust that the other really willed);
always the ritual stopped in the act of killing
(never the admission either one had killed).
Always arrived at last with deathknell chimes;
never the luxury, now, to smile "Sometimes."
Never had lovers suffered so long or well;
always each understood the other had not.
Always their poems, though, trickled around this blood clot.
Never was never an always dependable hell.

PHOBOPHILIA

Do you smell smoke?
If you don't, it's not
because a tenement isn't burning—
down the street, in Derry, Beirut, or San Salvador.

Did you just hear a scream?
If you didn't, it's not
because a woman wasn't raped
since I asked if you smelled smoke.

Did you notice anything funny
about the three men across the street
watching as you came in?
If you didn't, there's nothing
to laugh about.

Three out of four agor-
aphobiacs
seem to be women. Agoraphobia
means, simply, fear of
leaving one's home (or sometimes
one's room) and also means fear
of open or public places—
like the street or supermarket or movie theater,
playground or newsstand or subway or bar.
Three out of four.

This is the most common phobia,
they say, among women. It's the one I
don't share, used as I am
to leaving my clearest messages in open
or public places, such as poems
like last desperate biophide notes.
More and more what I fear
is the coming or being home, safe

where the silence, not walls, may close in,
or the heights be eroded or
the floors themselves under one's feet burst
into flame.

Those other phobias—such as anxiety at
certain elements (water or fire), or alarm
at particular animals (dogs, cats, strange men),
or terror at heights, depths, enclosed places—
these are more common, especially to women,
than agoraphobia, which means consequently
we have no hard
statistical data on them.
They are more integrated through daily living,
better clenched, sweatily, in the palm. They
need not paralyze the phobic, are less drastic
and so less reported. Many claustrophobiacs,
for instance, are in the closet.

But less drastic? Myself, as I grow
older, I smell smoke more often. I've become
a quite keen smeller of smoke these days.
In the middle of the night I rise
to check the gas jets, the fireplace, the boiler.
I keep flashing out of the corner
of my mind on flames
beside the bed *too late oh now too late*
or dancing along the beams *the ceiling's
caving oh my god* or puffing like cumulus
kumquat-colored clouds along the wings
of the planes that I, like a doomed Dutchwoman, fly
—always barring the
barring the
like a wall of red roar, a wind-
tunnel oven barring
the door.

Reincarniacs among you will assume
this is because I was burned at the stake—not once

but perhaps again and again until embers
still glow in my skull's milkglass globe, or crackle
each knuckle or flicker each cell from red to white
bloodheat or smoulder discreet at the marrow
to mirror internally what my charred bones
can no longer feel. Believe what you will.
I am done with simplifications.

Analysands among you will sift
for the burnt child in my past who
(literally) never was there. Believe
what you will. I am done with neat formulae.

Pragmatists among you might just note
that I live in a hundred-year-old tinder box
near a slum where junkies and bums patrol
deserted buildings, looking for places to light
inside campfires, keep warm. Or
that a firehouse clangs regularly, one block
away. Or that the flue in the fireplace
is almost as temperamental as the runaway
oven or recalcitrant wiring or
cunningly antique gas heaters who hiccup
and belch like a tragic Greek chorus,
its members all cloned from W. C. Fields.
The wretched of the hearth indeed.

A pragmatist just might discern
the dishes still ticking, the clocks
to be laundered, the statues of goddesses
melting before such banked heat as the heart's
wild denial of all my mere mortal humanity:
an arson so simple we have no statistical
data on its daily practice.

A pragmatist just might be getting somewhere
by inquiring as to the reasons, objective,
for why I haunt the dark
rooms, touching lightly the gas jets, sniffing

the ashes, disbelieving assurances no matter
how patronizing, watching the cats (my reality-checks).

As for flying, it used to delight me.
I've done it too much. And I'm done for.
It's bound to end badly
unless I can learn not to care.

What I care for increasingly, though,
is my phobia wisdom: getting to know
all my phobias, getting to hope they like me.

They are radical groundings
of abstract and liberal paranoid theory.
They are my practice. They are
rehearsals—not, as is thought, spokes
to be touched, or cracks in the sidewalk
which must be avoided.
They hone my technique.
They accustom my waking.
They array my going forth like a bride.

Are your palms getting sweaty?
Did you just hear a scream?
Do you smell someone burning?

THE RUINING OF THE WORK

(for Kenneth Pitchford)

"When once there awakens an apprehension of love's proper
dialectic, an apprehension of its pathological struggle, of its
relation to the ethical, to the religious, verily one will not
have need of hard-hearted fathers or ladies' bowers or
enchanted princesses or ogres and monsters in order to give
love plenty to do."

Either/Or,
Søren Kierkegaard

1

In the precision of this moment's space
I am loving you as if I were free to love
careless of cost, caste, or whatever I might save
instead: time, energy, soul, face.
To alter when it alteration needs,
there lies true love, which winningly dare lose
nothing but the apathy that feeds
our kiss, blood in the mouth, at the lips. But whose?
That neither can tell at last—this is the grace
peculiar to those like us who, stubborn, live
beyond what each fixed bloodless day impedes.
Myself so chosen, by this choice I choose:
watching, through such a depth and breadth and height,
god wear your features to tolerate my sight.

2

Clearly no unicorn could recognize the creature
silvering through the frame. That is the point.
No life-and-death courtship skills
of spider virtuosi could be other
than a Bosch hallucination, unsentimental
as porpoises are purposeless. They do not smile.

Forgive me my improvisations, world,
and lead me not into another broken covenant,
missed rendezvous, ersatz annunciation—
for I admit obsession with the theme
of radical exogamy, as if that rune
could spell our way
across the barriers of species
much less those of consciousness:

Beast and beauty, ondine and knight,
princess and frog, boy and dolphine,
swanqueen and prince, mermaid and merman
(blind to each other for some human sake)
—legends of an alien love
impossibly risked through broken spells, through
grief, betrayal, forgetfulness,
united by death, or magic.

Seascape, sandscape, inscape,
wherever we meet, you and I
twin fast but not the same, a spell
we can no longer even name
through salt-starched lips.

      Give me to drink, gasps one.

      I am drowning, the other replies.

3
Not to disown the dolphin;
still, one must fathom the predators
who claim to dive for greater depths: the stalkers
whose teeth jag backward toward the gullet,
who use proximity and speed and give off strings
of bluish light as they escort their prey;
and the ambushers, like anglerfish, who barely move
for weeks, waiting at levels
specified by dense cold and enormous pressure.

Always to be swimming against the tide?

>One woman says, "I left him when I thought
>I might be dying. And then I turned out healthy,
>after all." Another smiles, "I did it *for* him;
>he seemed unable to move." A third recites how long
>it had been coming, how inevitable, what good friends
>they are now. Fourteen years. Twenty-three years. Seven years.
>Insufficient pressure. Still others, with children,
>fossils of love like prehistoric aquan skeletons
>turned up in desert canyons. One mother snarls
>how much she hates his gestures
>on her daughter's hands. Another shrugs,
>"My children have lost an older brother, not
>a father."
>   And a woman whose love survived
>lynch mobs now reads her new poems
>about the energy of anger in a weary voice.
>Each of them speaks of his dependence, his depression.
>All of them touch on silence, cold, enormous pressure.

4
Opportunities for mating at such depths are rare.
Consequently, an angler male's sole function is
reproduction. He develops
no extensive feeding apparatus. Instead,
he finds an angler female, who is fifty times his size,
and attaches himself anywhere on her body
by sinking his teeth into her flesh.
Their tissues fuse permanently,
the body of the male degenerating until
he has become testes attached to the female,
nourished by his host's bloodstream.

5
Not only the marriages. Not only the male and female.
Plato of the *Phaedrus* knew: "As wolves
love lambs, so lovers love their loves."

Here is a woman shocked to find herself
fallen out of love with one whose coppery hair,
she'd once claimed, could electrify the dead.
Here is a woman who carries a gun
for protection against the woman for whose
protection she purchased the gun.
Here is another who recites how
long it had been coming, how inevitable,
what good friends they are now. Here
is a woman who grieves she has little power
and less hope, and she will sleep alone from here on in.
Here is a woman who smells of cedar, whose movements
are wooden, who blinks at the light,
and here is the woman she used to love,
who lied to herself, called the other a liar, then left
for a daughterly person more honest to lie with.
Each one pronounces on growth and selfhood—
the words bubbling up from a distance
nobody mentions. Nobody mentions
the silence, the cold, or the pressure.

At least the stomias, who are stalking predators,
encase themselves entirely in gelatinous sheaths
within which they wear reddish flecks:
luminous tissue that silhouettes each fish.
These lighted profiles empower the female and the male
to recognize each other
at such bathypelagic depths.

    6
For what human sake
this pathological struggle
through devotion
               toward praise?
Should we love
as if we were free to
love what scales would fall from our eyes?
Or have we already evolved

to this thetical jungle in which
all my claws grow back?

7

Always to be bent into the wind?
Always to be guilty of judgment,
anointed for damnation?

Blasphemy
and transcendence, you once wrote,
outrace each other to the same summit.

Around us the air grows thinner,
sifted with rock powdering from where we stood
just sentences ago. Beloved
feathered friends come all unstuck
like Icari and drop away.
Each time the silence undulates between us,
each time you freeze or my face flattens
with the pressure
something is risked that had been safe before
I held your breath in silver lungs.
The trust is little, the time less.
What fools would brave such cowardice?
Why is there such a lightness in this climb
like the temptation of a blessing
sweet as the Mexican marzipan skulls
showered on children at each winter's coming?

8

The separation and dissolution
of substance forms the test of alchemy, that moment
when base metal is reduced to chaos
so the higher spirit may melt into it,
the precision of that moment when the mind
frees itself from all routine.

This phase alchemists call
The Ruining of The Work
or The Abyss.

Only from such ruin, they say, can greatness come.

9

Give me a sign, I cried aloud,
while Pachelbel's stately canon built
its harmonic mockery of yearning,
a record of broken spells and covenants,
missed rendezvous, regret.

Messages come when most despaired of.
Something in *me* still thinks you are
a child like Blake, unscarred,
perfect as the child like Blake
something in me
still thinks *I* am.

This then would be
where we arch toward each other
through fathoms of sunlight, our bodies luminous
with recognition, our laughter loud, our skins
hot with a red-flecked radiance—
grave, holy twins
who have no need of you or me.
We are mere petals who drift
to the meadowfloor from their blossoming armloads,
we are the stories they tell for amusement,
the pets they keep, enchanted, in an ocean tank
or cage of air. We are the hammered gold
masks they wear to feel clownish or tragic.
We are their hide-and-seek games.

10

And did you think we would not still be lovers?
Dared you assume these hands, fouled with the stain

of all our battles, would not run blisters
to rend the veil between your face and mine?
Our lives bloom wild until our deaths grow ripe,
that's all. Spine against spine, stiff with fear
we drag our matter after mind. To stop
now is not in us. What we require
is everything, as always: the lineaments of desire.
Pledge me the old exposure in your eyes.
Such terms at worst are temporary where
lost lovers would direct our way
into the current. Love, give me your hand.
You and I alone know where we stand.

THREE

THE DUEL: A MASQUE

(for Gloria Steinem)

I

(Stage is in total darkness. From opposite sides of the stage area, out of the darkness, two voices call.)

HE

Give me to drink! gasps one.

SHE

I am drowning, the other replies.

(Two large masks begin to glimmer as the lights come up slowly in two pin-spots. The masks should be oversize, giving the impression of ritual masks, complete face coverings, but held, not worn. Each can be impaled—or give that impression—on a stick which the actor holds in front of herself/himself or tilts sideways as the situation arises, or holds far in front of the body, or drops to the side, etc. HE has the gold mask, SHE the silver. The features of the masks should otherwise be identical, however, and with open eyes through which the actors can see, and lips parted in a mystical buddha sneer. The masks now face the audience and, since the pin-spots are focused on them, we should ideally not be able to see the bodies of the actors behind/holding them. The actors, to facilitate this, should wear all-black clothing, identical leotards, black gloves. Their voices speak from behind the masks unless otherwise noted.)

SHE

What can we do? It's serious this time.

HE

When has it ever not been serious?

SHE

Whenever one of us held all the power,
the other all the understanding. Then.

HE

It's never been that simple.

SHE

What makes you think
that's simple? Nothing could be more complicated!

HE

You play word games. Not even playfully,
at that. My god, the melodrama of
"It's serious this time." I can't believe it!
We can't start this way! You must see that.

SHE

If I play word games it's because I'm forced
to use your words. I don't know what *my* language
is, or where it starts and yours might end.
I can't tell which of us is silent anymore.

HE

Oh I'm the one who's silent. Bet on that.

SHE

If so, it's your idea of some penance
for the years of bottling up my rage—
a penance like revenge.

HE

I don't suppose
it could be that I'm bottling up *my* rage?

SHE

Oh yes, this is a vintage year for that.
It's a performance I just marvel at:
your rendering of The Virtuoso Sulk.
Pure genius, first-rate, worthy of Achilles
in his tent, the real thing.

HE

You never
sulk, I see. I must be misidenti-
fying your deep existential *angst*.

SHE

Come off it, I'm talking about how you've perfected
your remoteness. God, the times I've tried to
penetrate that unlistening, unwatchful, any-
where-but-here-centering attention you
withdraw from every act of warmth I offer,
every recognition I attempt—

HE

Marshmelodrama!

SHE

Out of your mouth it's passion;
out of my mouth, of course, it's melodrama.

HE

It's hardly my fault you can't tell the difference.

SHE

Oh I can tell the difference. You know
the saying: A man is ruthless when he buys
and sells whole continents; a woman's ruthless
when she lets you hang on hold.

HE

You have it neatly planned, don't you? You give
yourself the best lines, too.

SHE

My dear, I can't
write your lines for you.

HE

You self-deluding hypocrite!
As if you hadn't censored and rewritten
them for a decade! As if, in reparation
for all the ages I had power over you,
you haven't power now—real power—over me.

SHE

The role-reversal trap? Isn't that
unworthy of your intelligence, my love?
The clever rumor Rome fell in a day?
Is it my fault that you've been wallowing in
the passive-aggressive radiance of The Zomboid
Phase all men with any feminist conscious-
ness seem to go through? What a choice: cruelty
or catatonia! When will you take
responsibility for your own life?

HE

How your demands do change! I've walked across
whole deserts of guilt on which I'd raped you and
denied you, enslaved and sold and silenced you,
claiming to love you all the while, walked
   (*His mask is beginning to slip slightly and as it tilts we glimpse a
   slice of his real face, tortured, behind it.*)
through a hell of guilt to reach some vague oasis
you promised glimmering on some found horizon,
if I could learn what love was. And what I learned
was this, precisely: that my life was yours.
Owed. But beyond that, given. Willingly.
   (HE *fixes the mask firmly upright again; his face is covered once
   more.*)
Fool! All this so you could change the rules
and throw it back?

SHE

         I said *responsibility.*
I said nothing about a debt or gift
of lives—that's deadly. You always overstate so.
Don't you understand I never meant
for you to leap to the burden of all history?
That's too vast—and too convenient. I've learned
to recognize armies and priesthoods, andro-
cratic governments, seducers, slavers.
It's when my own twin brother rapes, or when
my son falls silent in defense of truth,
or when my father turns his face from me,
or when my lover claims he's given me
his life—then I'm undone, done in, done for.
   (*Her mask has been slipping gradually during the last sentence;
   now we can see a slice of her face comparable to what we saw of
   his, and equally grief-stricken.*)
You make a gift into another job.
I cannot take responsibility
for your life, too. I have my own—

HE

(*Mask tilted, face half-exposed:*)
                                    You haven't
made me take responsibility
for yours, in waiting so actively for me
to change, then? In waiting so expertly *for* me
to turn "responsible"? Somewhere here
in all these snarls you must—

SHE

(*Mask tilted, face half-exposed:*)
                                    —take the respons-
ibility for *my* own life, yes.
And with no denial anywhere,
even of you. Even if you deny
us both just that.

HE

(HE *snaps his mask upright, covering his face.*)
                        I deny nothing nothing!
Let tribunals of women find me guilty
of whatever you accuse! Their judgment
won't be half so severe as mine.

SHE

(SHE *snaps her mask upright, too.*)
                                    Grandiose
one-upmanship to the very end, as always.

HE

(*Mask tilted, face half-exposed:*)
Look, can't we escape this? Can't we just be
a little happy? I'm still inside here, loving you,
all of my shreds drawn like bright filings toward
the force of you. We haven't got forever.

SHE

We have eternity, I'm afraid.

HE

The hell
we do—

SHE

I mean in one form or another.

HE

(*Mask upright:*)
You can say that because you're ten years younger.

SHE

I can say that because I'm trying to heave us
up from stereotypes into archetypes, darling.
(*Her mask slips halfway.*)
And because I'm here, too, inside
here, still loving you with all the furious
will that I first felt when I was yet
a girl and you stood lean and tense in khakis
and a white shirt by my mother's piano
and smoked a pipe and watched me through your narrowed
eyes between pipe puffs and talked to me
about Chopin and Sand. My god. You stood
for freedom then.
(*Sadly, but not yet masking:*)
That was before you turned—
you turned into my mother in my dreams.

HE

Did it never occur to you that I
did precisely that in order to

HE (cont'd.)

protect you from realizing just
how much you've turned into her all yourself?

SHE

(*Snapping her mask upright:*)
You know, you do know how to hurt, don't you?

HE

(*Mask full off in a sudden gesture; his face in profile toward her:*)
I didn't mean—

SHE

—*I* mean what you mean not
to mean: the quick deep lethal stab
as well as the long slow bloodsucking type wound
you've skillfully inflicted on me now
(*His mask snaps back up.*)
for years. No holds barred, then. The wars you've waged
against me, you and your kind, with weapons of steel
and flesh and ridicule and lust and pity—
your occupation and preoccupation
all the same, all one your means and meanings.

HE

How can we possibly begin afresh
if you insist on going over and over—

SHE

—what gets forgotten instantly? Lost
the second I don't nag it into being?
What goes directly from the category

SHE (cont'd.)

of Unspeakable to that of Boring,
without passing through mere Comprehension?
My tedious old suffering! It's such
an absent-minded telling of beads, a grocery
list: detergent, olive oil, foot bindings,
toothpaste, safety blades (for the legs? the armpits?
the jugular? the clitoris?), spermi-
cidal jelly, cat food, eggs . . .

HE

We know this.
We've spent years learning this. We've spent lives
carving those initials in our flesh.
Do you remember nothing else? Not
the time I was sobbing with grief in your arms at just
these insights, and you kept saying, "Never mind
the past, my love. There's time to change. The world
lies all before us, ours to choose for real,
at last. Don't look backwards, love," you said.

SHE

That was in another act, when you
were being Orpheus, and I was being dead.

(*Blackout.*)

II

(*About five-second lapses occur in the blackouts, and then the
pin-spots should come up swiftly. Time lapse can be longer if and
when needed for actors to rearrange their positions or masks,
but the pacing should be sharp.*)

HE

(*Totally unmasked, full face to the audience:*)
Are you in there?

SHE

(*Masked:*)
                    Are you?

HE

                              Ah, if you
would ever answer simply: Yes . . .
          (HE *masks.* SHE *unmasks, completely, full face to the audience. His
          face is now completely covered.*)

SHE

                              Are you
in there?

HE

Of course. Where else would I be?

SHE

                                        Ah,
if you would ever answer simply: Yes . . .

(*Blackout.*)

III

(*Pin-spots up, on the masks, held toward each other in profile,
while another pair of spots highlights the actors' faces, turned full
to the audience.*)

SHE

If you're not in there, no god is possible.

HE

If you're in there, no god is necessary.

(*Blackout.*)

IV

(*Lights up as before. This time they both are unmasked, the masks held before them at waist-level, or to one side.*)

HE

How beautiful you are, naked like that.
    (SHE *says nothing, but confusion passes over her face, and she suddenly snaps her mask up into place before it. Blackout.*)

V

(*Lights up, as before. Both unmasked, as before.*)

SHE

What's wrong? Are you angry at me? Answer me.

HE

    (*Raising his mask as he speaks:*)
No. Don't keep asking. I'm all right. Leave
me alone. Why do you insist I'm angry?

(*Blackout.*)

VI

(Lights up. Both unmasked. Direct address to one another.)

HE

Listen, there's something missing here. We can't
do this without the child!

SHE

Why not? Why can't we?
We have at other times. After all the child
wasn't there to start with, you recall.

HE

But the child's presence alters everything.

SHE

No, it sharpens everything, but changes
nothing. Certainly not this. Besides,
I have . . . personal problems about child actors.

HE

But I can't just pretend no child exists!

SHE

Men have managed to do exactly that
for centuries. Try to descend, dear,
to the occasion. I'm sure you'll manage. Positions,
please. Draw your mask, if you insist.

HE

(Begins to raise his mask:)
You're avoiding reality. I don't
think that's what could be called "responsible."

SHE

(Begins to raise her mask:)
You're avoiding the issue. And using the child
to do it. I don't think *that's* responsible.
Besides, this is between you and me
and always has been.
    (Pause.)
                    Always.
    (Pause.)
                       Hasn't it?

(Both their masks snap up into place. Blackout.)

VII

(Lights up, both fully masked.)

SHE

How can you wear at once my child's face
and the expression of my latest assassin
who leaves his promises taped to my door each dawn?

HE

Why do you know those two outlines best?
How much of my mask was sculpted by your hands?

SHE

What are the planes and folds and secret places,
then, of that face, which face, beneath the ones
you claim you turn, unfolding, plain, to me?

HE

Feel which is alive. There are places in me
you have never touched—beyond the strength
you fear, the weakness you despise. Beyond.

SHE

The woman capable of reaching them
lived in another country, and is dead.
Wasn't her death-mask sculpted by your hands?
As for this mother, this target, this woman, as for
me, my grasp of you exceeds her reach.

(*Blackout.*)

VIII

(*Lights up.* SHE *is unmasked.* HE *is masked.*)

SHE

Who are you?

HE

Whoever you want me to be.

SHE

That
is every kind of lie.

HE

Then lie with me,
my love.

SHE

There it is at last: the truth.

(SHE *snaps up her mask;* HE *lowers his completely.*)

HE

Who are you?

SHE

Someone who mixes up loving
you with god.

HE

But I know you're an atheist.

SHE

Exactly. That's the problem. Devout, lapsed,
apostate, and pharisaical.

HE

No wonder your saving grace is being damned.

(*Blackout.*)

IX

(*Lights up.* HE *is turned upstage, back to the audience. We cannot
see whether or not* HE *is masked.* SHE *is masked.*)

HE

Oh come, forgodsake. Look. We could be sane,
just for a little while, we could be happy.
Look. There, how the sunlight streams like love.
See where our own dense bodies are netted in shadow
only as a way to outline how
flesh swims surrounded by displaced but still
delineating love. We could be happy.

SHE

(*Slowly, warily, as* SHE *jitters her mask on and off during the next
speeches:*)
How can I trust you? If I could just believe . . .
Are you smiling?

HE

(*Not turning:*)
See, out there, only
follow me and—

SHE

Can I believe you? What—
what is your face like? What is your expression?
Turn and let me see you.

HE

I dare not turn
for fear of losing you. Look where I'm looking.
Fix your eyes on what lies just ahead.

SHE

Are your cheeks wet? Is your jaw clenched? Are you
perspiring? Turn. I want to see your face.

HE

Don't ask this of us. Don't do this to us.

SHE

Are you biting your tongue? Are you blinking fast? I must know
if you're lying. I must know if the mask is on or not.
I must know—

HE

No! Must you destroy us?
Depend on *me,* for once! Trust me! Trust
my voice. Hear me!

SHE

Your voice falls on deaf ears.
If I can look in your eyes, I'll know. I'll know
if it's you—or if it's your articulate mask.
Turn to me. Let me see your face.

HE

If
I didn't love you, I could turn!

SHE

I don't
know who is saying that!
    (*By now* SHE *has forgotten her own mask completely; it dangles
    by her side.*)
        Why should love fear
to show its face? Turn!

    (HE *very slowly begins to turn toward her, but before the audience
    can see whether or not* HE *is masked,* SHE *exhales a long breath,*

like a gasp or sigh, and her spotlight swiftly fades to darkness, then blackout. Instantly, his spotlight also blacks out. In total darkness, we hear him cry out:)

HE

Eurydice!

X

(Lights up on both. HE *is masked.* SHE *is unmasked.)*

HE

Why did you fade from me?

SHE

Are you so sure
I did?

HE

What did you see? Me? Or the mask?
Let me see what you saw.

SHE

(Snaps up her mask.)
You, of course.

(Blackout.)

XI

(Lights up on only one character. SHE *is unmasked, but her mask*

has assumed a persona of its own and SHE *is in dialogue with it.*
They face one another. The voice of the mask can be performed
by another actress, or can be pre-taped for dialogue with the ac-
tress on stage, by herself, in her own voice.)

MASK VOICE

He's never really looked at you. He has
refused to see you. He claims you are Euryd-
ice and it would kill you. He claims you are
Medusa and it would kill *him.* There's always some
excuse. What is he afraid of seeing?
Or what is he afraid you'll see when he does?

SHE

No, you don't understand. You simplify . . .

MASK VOICE

I understand. It's simple, simpleton.
It's all because you've ceased to be his mirror—

SHE

No! It's all because I *am* his mirror—
and he's mine. Oh, don't you see? The worst,
most secret fear is not that we are different,
not The Other, but The Same. The terror
of life itself Oneface—no more camouflage,
no screen, nothing lost in the translation.
The terror of the moment when a somatic
cell doesn't know itself as different
from a genetic cell. Heresy,
metastasy. An utterly alien Real.
Don't you see how such a fear dwarfs
the mere anxiety that male and female,
white and black, master and slave, myth
and history, any and any, are not the same?

MASK VOICE

They're *not* the same. My poor blank featureless sister,
how you need me. You *are* his mirror, yes,
and a magnifying one at that. But
he's not yours. You haunt his surfaces
in vain, seeking your image: an undead, damned,
lost soul. Look to me to find your face.

SHE

You're wrong. You may be right for now; you're wrong
for ever. You've never really looked at me
yourself. I need no mirrors, after all. It's not
to see myself in everything I want
but to find everything at home in me.

MASK VOICE

Ultimate nurturance! You merely would
domesticate the universe! That's
the pretentious luxury of those who win
a revolution. Well? Win it first, then!

SHE

I'm tired of fighting. It has been sixteen
thousand, four hundred and twenty-seven years,
five months, eight weeks, three days, six hours, and
. . . eleven minutes nineteen seconds.

MASK VOICE

                              Stop
fighting, then. Retire into the shapes
I offer you. They're yours. Abandon him.

SHE

Leave me. Let me go barefaced as a truth.

MASK VOICE

I'll leave you when you leave him. Not before.

SHE

*(Turns downstage away from the mask, but then holds it behind
her back, so that the face of the mask appears over her own
shoulder, behind her.)*
Blesséd Saint Heloise of the Roseate Hell,
pray for me. Look how I alone sanctify
your name, in the teeth of the lackloves and the inquisitors.
Holy Saint Heloise, who knew, anathema,
the erotic desire for god *now*, in *this* world,
pray for me. Heloise, blesséd heretic whose god
in yourself deosexually sought out its own divine self
through Peter Abelard, lover and fool, who never
understood, or if he did, denied you,
pray for me. Saint Heloise, pray for me
because, surrounded by women, you could not see
yourself. Saint Heloise, pray for me,
for you too were cursed with capability
and, what is worse, compassion for his sin:
the cunning that pretends him blessed with wise
incompetence. Saint Heloise, who saw
how he was tricked into thinking himself unmanned
for love of you, for love, pray for him.
Saint Heloise, who understood his pain,
withdrawal, and bitterness at both; who shared
my guilt, and my resentment of my guilt,
pray for us. Saint Heloise, who felt
the stigma of curséd understanding in
the face of action, help me to act. Heloise,
who art in Hell with Abelard, pray for us.
Blesséd Holy Heloise, pray for us both—
now and at the hour of our birth.

(Blackout.)

XII

(Lights up on only one character. HE *is unmasked.)*

HE

The space between. The dish in which the culture
grows. One says, Don't. The other continues.
A way of walking, a tone of voice, a pillow
left casually in the middle of the bed.
Your fingers running nervously through your hair.
The tightness at your mouth, compressing into
silence what is clearly said. Linguistic
analyses, rosetta stones, graffiti,
signals, messages, markings, codes, clues, poems.

(Light fades down on him, and HE *raises his mask. Light comes up
on her;* SHE *is unmasked.)*

SHE

Either I am justified in my
demands and he, in his refusal or
his inability to meet them, means
to destroy me . . . or . . . he really loves me
and would change even far more than he
already has—if only my demands
weren't so thoroughly unfair and, yes,
insane. A way of folding clothes. A way
of using illness. The peculiar manner
of pushing out the lower lip in hatred.
  (Turning to him, or toward his direction:)
The expertise with which you can pretend
not to hear the nightmares I pretend
to have, while both of us pretend we're sleeping.
  *(*SHE *turns back and raises her mask. Blackout.)*

XIII

(Lights up on both characters, unmasked.)

HE

Are you implying that you want to play
it out as farce, then?

SHE

> When has it ever not
been farce?

HE

> When it's been tragedy, that's when.
When one of us dies. When we are given the
enchanting choice of two scenarios for
the lovers/artists team: *The Red Shoes,* where
you get to jump in front of a train and die
for the sake of my career—or *A Star Is Born,*
where I get to walk into the sea and drown
so as not to impede your success.

SHE

> That isn't farce?

(Both raise their masks.)

HE

All evening long. You kept on interrupting
me all evening long! I couldn't believe it!

SHE

We went over that last night when we got home.
I *said* that I was sorry.

HE

But you always
say that off the top, without much feeling.
It doesn't cost you a goddamned thing. "I'm sorry."
Just like that. To wriggle off the hook,
co-opt all criticism before it can be
anywhere near fully aired. Damned clever!

SHE

Don't yell at me.

HE

(*Yelling:*)
Why in hell did you
keep interrupting me?
(*Then, in a calm voice:*)
And I'm not yelling.

SHE

Because, if you must know, you'd rambled on
with great enthusiasm while everyone else's
eyes glazed over, so after a millennium
I took mercy on us all. I in-
terrupted. I'd rather look like a harpy than have you
look like an ass.

HE

Aren't we the perfect little
martyr! Your defenses are incredible.

SHE

They better be, to cope with your offences.
You know you were boring and couldn't stop

SHE (cont'd.)

and needed to be interrupted, too. That's why
you're pissed at me, in fact.

HE

How dare you presume—

SHE

Sorry to interrupt, dear, but that's salt,
not sugar, you've just poured into your coffee.

(*Blackout.*)

XIV

(*Lights up on only one character.* HE *is unmasked, but in dialogue
with his mask, as* SHE *was with hers earlier. The voice of the mask
can be pre-recorded by the same actor, or played by another actor.
The mask and the character face each other, in profile to the audi-
ence.*)

MASK VOICE

She's never loved you, idiot. She's only
interested in breaking you, the bitch.
She's power-crazy. Hasn't your life become
one round of dishes, laundry, head- and back-aches,
sleepless sexless nights, depression? Then who's
the housewife, kiddo, hmmm?

HE

No, you don't
understand. You simplify . . .

MASK VOICE

I understand. She wants to flay you for a rug,
that's what.

HE

No! It's you she wants to flay—
from me. It's you, it's you she wants to shatter
along with those formations beaded, crusted,
on *her* face. I know her. I know how
she knows me. It's infinite regress of recognition,
only forward. Or it could be. Except
for cowardice in our outfacing what lies
lie before us. Except for saving face.

MASK VOICE

Men think you're nuts, you know. And here's the kicker:
so do women.

HE

I've learned not to care
much about that.

MASK VOICE

And so does she, old buddy.
There's your rub.

HE

If she thinks I'm mad, well,
it's her own madness showing. Or else what
she sees as my own madness looks like you.

MASK VOICE

My poor defenseless moron of a brother,
how you need me. She's cut you adrift out in the sea
of her self-centeredness and you with nothing
but the splintered raft of your desire
to cling to. Look at me! I can return
you to your manly self!

HE

I've tried that. For many
years, in fact. The truth is that you never
gave me half so much as did this stranger—

MASK VOICE

—or asked so damned much in return!

HE

                          That's right!
Asked what I wanted most to have required
of me, as fully human.

MASK VOICE

                  Awwww. Opposites
attract? The magic of complement? Listen,
that kind of generous gesture is best made
from a position of unimpeachable strength.

HE

I'm tired of fighting. It's been god-knows-how-many
thousand years.

MASK VOICE

       Stop fighting, then, and crush her
utterly by turning into me.

HE

       Leave me.
You fill my dreams no longer.

MASK VOICE

       I'll fill your nightmares,
then. If her shapes' greed will lend me room.

HE

*(Turns downstage away from the mask, but holds it behind his
back so that the mask-face appears over his own shoulder.)*
Where is the meditation for a mind
whose worship is unacceptable? Whose love
is not enough, whose daily tasks still
not enough, whose energy sloughs
like flaked skin all unloved down to inertia?
I, who would be to her all passion, movement,
grace, desire, go gross with duty like
a frog prince in his spell—waiting to be
recognized and kissed into myself.
With each croak, do I hold her back? Is this
some ultimate discourtesy to her?
Would the great act of love be then to force her
so away from me that she would not
remember how she ever could have loved me?
Does such a sacrifice lie in me? Or does it
lie in fact so deep that I can never
be quite sure of what it means, or who
it means to save, free, save from whom?
She speaks of my dependence—this woman who sees
our human love as a religious act—

HE (cont'd.)

my dependence? God's dead, or female, or not yet
born; certainly not me, defiantly
mortal, soon old, ill, dying, and soon dead.
And all those poems unwritten for dishes done
and dirtied and done again and silences
and effort. Wasted. An expense of passion
in a caste of shame. Who am I, anyway?
Who is this man she will not, will not leave
in peace? How can I love the very one
who made me all-suspicious of my loving,
and of her? How can I not love someone
who so loved me she dared even that?

(*Blackout.*)

XV

(*Lights come up on both characters, both masked.*)

HE

Have the women come to a verdict, then?

SHE

Yes.
Androcide. Would you like a snack?

HE

No,
thank you. Was the count . . . unanimous?

SHE

But for one vote.

HE

I see.

SHE

Do you?

HE

(*Shouting, as his mask tilts slightly upward, as if calling out:*)
You can come and get her now! She's the traitor!

SHE

On the *first* ballot.

HE

Ah . . . Then we'd better
hurry, before they—

SHE

Now you see my point.
The urgency. It's serious this time.

HE

Do you have long enough to take that snack?

SHE

If we travel light.

HE

Clearly. But then
what about . . . ?
(HE *gestures toward the masks.*)

SHE

They can look after themselves.

(SHE *steps out from behind the gold mask we have come to think of as his, while at the same instant* HE *emerges from behind the silver mask we thought hers. They face one another and go off together, not touching, but also not taking their eyes off each other's faces. The lights fade to two dim pin-spots, one on each mask, left standing with their handles in holders, so that we see only the mask faces. Blackout.*)

Curtain.

FOUR

DOCUMENTARY

(Based on the documentary film *River of Sand*, by
Robert Gardner, a Phoenix Productions Film from
Harvard University.)

The Hamar of Southwest Ethiopia
are the subject.

But too much stands between
for understanding, between us and this
stone-age people—an alien tribe, a dying culture,
and a geographical distance great
even in these days of Concorde.

Still, she is—how old? Not an elder,
she has no standing as an elder: she's a woman.
There is nothing that does not come between us.

"One keeps going," she says, squatting,
brushing at the flies that return to her face.
"When a son is born, the father gives him a gun.
When a girl is born, the father gives her leg irons.
It's not just me." She laughs but never smiles.

"Your father wars and gives you away.
Nobody sees you. Where can you go?
You enter your husband's house a girlchild
with only your rings as your own: leg rings, rattling
arm rings. Your skirt is taken away.
In your newness you are afraid of him.
You become of his people." She says this.
I say, Everything stands surely
between us, you and I, we are not—

She describes a ceremony:
now he is old enough to beat women and girls,

to hunt, now he is a new man. Babies beat
dogs, men beat women; "cattle wear bells,
women wear bracelets, you are a rattle
in a new man's hand, you control yourself and go on."

All her front teeth have been torn out. "When
I was circumcised, you understand." She says
this, she uses the word "circumcision," not
clitoridectomy, not naming
how the sharpened shell carved out the clitoris,
the excision of pleasure, the scream
that is proof of womanhood, not speaking
the word "infibulation": the sewing up of the labia,
leaving one hole for urine and pus and menstrual fluid
to seep through, or the then forced
tearing open to ensure him virginity,
loyalty, tightness. She does not say this. I
say this, and I say, What more
could possibly stand between us, what—

>   the rattle of iron bracelets, *the rattle*
>   *"for decoration and for bondage"*
>   she says this
>   the rattle of teeth into a wooden bowl

"Women look best when scarred." She says
they say this. There are scars on her belly.
She says, "Women carry the scars earned by men
for killing an enemy. Men do not scarify themselves—
they build headdresses of clay and of ostrich plumes
and they decorate these, but men do not scar their own
flesh. It is for women to carry their scars."
She is actually bitter, she dares to be bitter,
she laughs and snarls at her own tribe,
at the camera, she rattles like a desert snake.

"You are beaten," she says. *You are*
>   *beaten as your mother was beaten.*
>   *You are ground beneath the grinding stone.*
>   The rattle

of small drums, the rattle of wire whips.
The crunch of sorghum on the grinding stone
the rhythm.
"*He is*

beating you even when he is not," she says.
"His whip is always in his hand, and when you run
he only sits. Where could you go?"
Everything stands everything between I am not

"You become reconciled, and that is that. Then
the husband will leave you alone." She says this aloud.
"Do women have erections or go cattle raiding
or hunting?" she laughs. "Do women have erections or kill? No,"
she rattles, "women work. Women kill lice
until the sun sets, that is how we raid. Women get wood
and go home, women haul water and work
the sorghum field. That is how we hunt.
You stay. You grind the sorghum stone,
                you are the grinding stone,
you touch your children and you stay."

Too much for understanding too
great a distance—

"Men own beehives and collect honey. The leg rings
of a woman are like new beehives in a tree: they look so fine
and new." She says they say this. She says,
                "*You become of his people. Nobody sees
                you. How can it be
                bad? Where can you go?*
Men sit on stools, drink from gourds.
Women sit on the ground. After the first birth
your husband will say, 'A child has come from between
us. Shall I then beat you forever?' "

Not her
I am not you
are not surely cannot be
we are

"Who does not
in this world practice slavery?"
She laughs, the toothless sophisticate.
"You touch the child, you stay."
Now he is old enough to beat women to show his love,
she unsmiles. *A woman may be whipped only*
by a man of the clan into which she will marry.
We are not savages, she rattles.

We are
not the subject, you and I. I say
this. We are not a stone-age people. We at least
try surely everything stands between

Men jump cows, drink blood, suck marrow,
pray for the desert flooding.
"May all be well," men say
and spit upon the ground to make it ripe.
Women are to look best when scarred, a woman
is to be resigned into freedom only when he cannot follow
her death because she is not
I am not
the subject

When you die they will butter your corpse
and fold it like a stillborn child into the hole.
Your husband's oldest brother leads the ritual,
and lays heavy stones across the grave. You will not
escape. Whips are cut
from the barasá tree and are strewn
above your body
to control your vengeance.
A kid is sacrificed, especially when
you die in childbirth.
Your corpse is buttered with blood.

You and I
everything stands I refuse
nothing not a stone age we are surely

"You are beaten as your mother was beaten," she sings.
> *You are ground beneath the grinding stone,*
> *you are sorghum and stone, it isn't just me,*
> *cattle wear bells, women wear irons, you*
> *control yourself and go on*

        The rattle of her voice,
the rattle of iron bracelets, of teeth
into a bowl of laughter, the rattle
of a desert snake, of shell against pelvic bone,
grain against stone. The rattle in the throat.

No   barrier.
Nothing stands between us.

        As your mother was beaten.
        As my mother was beaten.
No distance. No distance traveled?
Nothing stands behind us.

Who does not in this world practice slavery?
        No map, no model.
Nothing stands before us.

The Hamar of Southwest Ethiopia are
        not the subject.

AERIAL VIEW

(on a work by Katherine Kadish)

A woman is leaning out of the fog.

A woman is leaning on her elbow out of the fog by the side
of the road

A woman is lying leaning on her elbow waiting by the side
of the road

She must be a hitchhiker running away from home

She must be a whore, spread so seductively out

A woman is emerging through the mist, one hand touching
her genitals the other trying to give herself
support, leaning

She must have been raped and crawled to the side of the road
to try and flag down some help

She must be in labor, the baby coming before its time, out
there alone walking along the road

A woman is reclining, massive, chthonic goddess, norn, one
elbow resting on her mountain for a cushion, one
hand toying with the veil of her fog

A woman is floating sideways in out of time, now scaled small
as remembrance: a ghost, an old lover, a landscape,
a mother, a self

A woman is receding—or approaching—out of the sideways waltz
of color, her pale hair streams, her face is wet
with color, the mist does not delineate her features

She must be meeting someone

She must be an artist, lying back to gain perspective on a work
    she is painting which she thinks is an aerial landscape

She must be a poet, believing she's writing a poem about a painting
    of a woman emerging from a mist

She must be too distant to see whether woman or landscape
    is gesturing, painter or poet

We live this way—each blurring lyricism across her life with
    all craft's deliberation, high-riding broom
    and brush and pen so as not to hurtle
    downward into what we know, and die.

ELEGY

(for Florika, 1946–1979)

"Perfect the elegiac form—you'll need it, kid,"
I can almost hear her say, in that voice like a cello

in minor key, accented with slow ironies of language
from at least four different European countries

she had fled through, until she came to rest uneasily
at home here in the new world where she'd die.

But the cello was not her instrument—although toward the end
she played bass with a male jazz band, a joke

or curiosity until the audience heard
the strings like lovers strain to touch her fingers.

No, the violin had been her means of music,
Roumanian gypsy that she was, dark

greengold skin stretched like a tambourine across
the drum and cymbal bones of her percussive face.

Approximate, at least, the elegiac form,
even when bare facts, which look best in black,

describe better perhaps than poetry this full-term grief.
Nine months ago she died, in autumn, at the close

of the decade. Now, in late spring, I learn of it;
now she dies backward for me, a retrospective

from June receding, through months I thought her alive—if
I thought of her at all. It had been years

since we met, and when I saw her last she didn't
hear me call her name through traffic, but crossed

the intersection already buried in her own thoughts,
while the bus bore me away beyond her hearing.

Still, we were women of an age, though she seemed always
the elder—tall, slender, that mask of watered

silk shimmering tight across her luminous skull
so eager to show itself picked clean. Dear god, my sister,

is it fifteen years since we sat on the floor in that small room
in Judith's lower-east-side apartment, thirteen

of us, alone in the world and utterly unalike, except
for the music: women's voices, quietly telling

this one's pain, that one's humiliation, her fears,
my longings, your visions, our anger. What has died into rhetoric

lived in that room, drew its breath in terror to be born.
Not all the war-soaked battlefields of time

have seen such heroism as each woman risked
sitting on the floor in a circle, those Tuesday evenings.

Young and bitter, we wore our rage like cloaks of radiance.
Our very hems sparked energy, and we were gloved

and shod with laughter, acid laughter, wicked laughter,
armored with glee for all our dangerous plots.

I wonder in what plot you lie now—you, who had managed
to be a myth even while alive:

each of us misremembers her own version of you.
Judith always thought you were raised Catholic,

Peggy felt you were atheist and Marxist, I could swear
I recall some story of how you had been smuggled

out of a Roumanian Jewish ghetto while
the Nazi landlords were in charge, and how

you were a child prodigy who escaped your mother
after several nervous breakdowns. We agree,

however, on certain versions of our myth about you:
how you were forced to bed five days each month

with cramps so powerful they drove you to your knees,
despite all remedies devised; you who loved

word games almost as much as the violin you'd never
touch; you, who tried to make us understand

the force of your madness—that it was not glamorous,
not always a sign of political sanity,

not when words came gagging, landscapes flattened, toothed
doorways yawned, not when the violin played

by itself. You were "the invisible woman" in my poem.
You were the first woman I heard say

that oppression's greatest sin wasn't in refusing
to grant what was due, but in refusing to accept

what the oppressed could give. How many years had you spent
in asylums, how many years more would you spend,

before and after that clearing in the jungle of your nightmares,
that sunlit space where women's voices almost

convinced you to play again? In time, we went our ways,
keeping in touch, reconstructing our lives

as best we could, making ourselves and history
alone and with other women. I saw you a few times

to really talk, we spoke by phone, then less and less.
I heard you'd moved away, back home to Europe,

then back home here, then made your home in California.
I imagined things were bad: I heard about

a break-up with a man, a new man, then another.
You were on heavy drugs. You fought, and kicked

the habit. It fought back. You wanted no sisterhood.
Rumors? Projections? Additions to the myth?

What I will live with is: we failed you utterly.
This was not our fault; we were powerless to give.

This was our fault. It was our most oh grievous fault.
The very last I knew, you, who founded

the first "women's liberation band" we called it,
you were playing stoned on smack in a male

jazz combo, gigging one-night stands at seedy joints
in Oakland or L.A.—but trying to form a women's

string quartet in the afternoons. Damn you, Florika,
listen: Prokofiev's second violin concerto

is mourning for you on the phonograph, while I
write these words, stupidly crying at the typewriter

nine months after—what? the overdose? Too late
these tears, too late these words to play with now,

too late my second-guessing at your life or death,
too late to free the years of silence—no sweet

string rejoicing under your bow, no remedy
for the "incorrect" pain of your bleeding, no answer to madness,

no sound. We die each day in silence, hush, we're dying.
We dream each night a music we've never heard,

and now I'll dream your ghostly face white-wreathed in garlic
flowers. Yours was the wild hair streaming I wrote of,

yours were the castinets you gave my newborn child
—which I still have. Their click has chipped away

the paint—orange and blue—for a decade. That click
echoes through the silence like a clock.

You're dead, no longer one of us. You're dead. How dare you?
Wait—walk among us, haunt us, drive us sane.

I must perfect the elegiac form, I know,
for others will die, have died, are dying now,

all our female dead, their silence louder than a violin
could drown. Was this nausea the one you felt?

Look at these lines: awkward approximations of a form,
opportunistic usage of your death.

Let it all go then, including the temptation to see you
as a martyr, or even a casualty.

You were yourself, I need not make you into Woman.
This grief is for you alone, specific, personal.

Goodbye, my dear. Close the volcanic eyes that flickered
in that lovely face. Put the violin away now.

I stand above a grave I've never seen and pray,
but not for you. "Pray for the living," you laugh.

I pray: God damn all silences except those sweat-freshened
by making love or art or revolution.

WHITE SOUND

(for Jewell Parker Rhodes)

"It is not right
for mourning to enter a home of poetry."

Sappho

I

"Forgive me for not having heard
what your silence was saying more clearly;
I was busy calling you deaf."
—Those, the first words I wrote
on coming to this quiet place, lie
now at the bottom of the lake,
their ripples on the surface long since
stilled, the waterruffles having reached
the banks and scampered up in soundwaves
to shake themselves dry and, looking left and right,
move off toward the deeper woods.

I follow more slowly, picking my way
across ground-cover less grass than myrtle
flowering now white, now purple, between
columns of hemlock and white pine.
Each forsythia deafens with its exclusive claim
to be the burning bush: God in me! No,
me! No, God in me! The honeysuckle is fanatic,
a religious fundamentalist, not like the trillium,
which keeps to itself in stands of four or five,
each chaste bloom three-petaled and white
as white mint, each stem a slender green as green.

Behind me, pagan in the orchard,
apple-blossom boughs are studded with bees

who rise and settle, rise again and settle
like a pointillist lover repositioning an embrace
or like decorative hatpins tufted in yellowbrown velvet
stabbing their lace-pale cushion.

I am a city woman.

2

Metaphysician, heal thyself. Why should I
find it easier to grow *impatiens* on a
tarblistered roof than plant
words onto paper when there is no acid
in my soil? Ashamed of such excuses,
I watch the male cardinal smear wingspread-width
the spring sky with color red on blue fresh
from the art of Mycenaean Crete. It can be done.

Even for me, though, who give myself
airs of domesticity, these trails crunching
pleasantly underfoot feel a bit tame—
not like a seacoast eroding the heart,
or a city intersection. One day, the rain
seems to brighten a twilight, pearling
white drops thick from a thick white sky.
I walk through its beaded curtain

wearing sensible shoes, but I am
a city woman still. I hallucinate
the telephone. I dream I have missed a train.
I dream I am paralyzed from the neck down
because of an accident in a swimming pool
in which I was hit surprisingly hard with a
plastic toy. I dream I can no longer

tell the screams of a human from those of a jay:
streetcurses, brakesqueal, sirens,
the whining of a child, the sobs of a hostile lover,
dreams of real wilderness, all muffled

as if by a white-sound machine.
I dream I am a siren singing underwater,

having lured myself to death.

3
How dare we call the scream of a jay
its natural sound simply because

we've never heard it sing? Things happen
in translation. While artists work here, the death toll

mounts in Florida, where I was born—
black bodies falling like needles

from a white pine tree. A volcano erupts.
Nothing so pacified, inert, or tame

it can be trusted beyond a certain solstice
of gratuitous pain: the well-meant joke on sex or race

the *teller* can afford not to hear clearly,
all honorable men counting on laughter

to drown out the crude Polack strains
of a Chopin étude. If a woman paces

in her room, black fists clenched white
with anger; if a woman works in her cabin

defying terror to understand another
woman on her page; if a woman

stalks herself on canvas; if a woman
builds herself jade burial armor;

if a woman walks in the woods and walks
and walks and grinds her white forehead

against indifferent moss and weeps
and rages at such weeping, what does it mean?

If a woman falls in the forest and
no one hears, is there sound?

4

       There is a poem missing here,
       unlike the deliberate flaw the Navaho weaver
       leaves in her blanket—to let the soul out.
       Such a poem would be a luxury, a passion;
       it could afford trust, it could have something
       to do with love, but craftily. Or
       it could be raucous with humor—
       the special kind those who have so deplorably
       lost their sense of, have, when alone
       with one another. It could be a lament,
       frangible as a bird's egg, longing to break
       the silence. But it would sing, at least,
       the way an elegy might stretch its grief taut
       on a violin string, unafraid to mourn and still
       be beautiful. Such poems are rare.

       To be deflected from their making by pain
       or powerlessness is the greatest loss.
       To be deflected from their making by ignorance
       or power, by choice, might be the only sin.

       We settle for cheap grace too often.

5
I thought I had come to this place to stage
the mysteries as they once might have been
celebrated. I dream of having an audience
with the Three Norns—all dark-skinned women
laughing with love. I wonder
how could she have known, Demeter,
driving out of reality on the private road
in a blue car, looking older than her age.

"Remember this face"—holding out to me
  a wallet photograph of a young woman, blonde, blue-
  eyed. "My little girl," she says, her lips
  straight as the vital-signs signal of one dead.
"She disappeared ten days ago in front of this place.
  She took no clothes or anything she loved
  with her, so *she* was taken, somehow. She didn't just
  go, I mean." I look at her as if I have imagined her.
  I say, "How old—? I mean I'm sure she'll
  come back" and I'm lying. "Fifteen," she says.
  I think: Persephone, trim-ankled, gathering
  flowers. "She'll come back," I say, and reach
  through the rolled-down car window to touch
  the bony shoulder. I shouldn't have—it brings
  acidic tears to both of us. "If she's still
  alive," she answers, and bites the scab on her lip.
  Finally, I am silent. "I've put a tracer on her,"
  she whispers, and accelerates off down the road.

Sweet god Demeter I never meant to meet you
  in these woods Momma I never thought you were
  still looking—for she is lost to you, lost,
  whether she went willingly or was dragged,
  whether she thought him attractive
  or scary, whether the glitter
  was in his eyes or along the edge of something
  metal he pulled from his pocket. And
  why ask me? Why rendezvous with me of all people
  here the fool out walking in the brightening rain,
  pretending I am not a city woman, not a white
  woman, not a woman, just a poet?

6
Things die even if left where they belong—
  which is obvious, but politics can't solve that.
  Cut flowers in the city seem naturally
  short-lived, but perish almost as quickly unplucked.
  Already the apple-blossoms have disappeared,

the forsythia bushes gone bare green,
the trillium focusing inward to the prophesied
red berry of late summer. The lilacs lavish and
are gone; narcissi, columbine, wild mustard
stand and die; the lily-of-the-valley, bridal veil,
a violet or two must tide us over until roses.
I am not such a city woman I cannot celebrate
whatever I can—although the scream
that last drew me out with robe and flashlight
into the night, I knew was animal: something
trapped, devouring or being devoured.

Who said these trails were tame?
Who said however loud (or still thinks,
whispering) that genius finds itself
uncomfortable wearing certain shades of skin,
finds unreconcilable clitoris and brain
for habitation? Who welcomed mourning
into the house of poetry?

What we deny, denies us.
What we make live in art denies us
if the blood spilled to it is anyone's
but our own. All else is white sound,
drowning what we might have sung, had we
but dared to use the skill I fear as much
as you do: to recognize that we are doomed
together—human, artists, all

mad atheists insatiable for god.

THE FALL OF A SPARROW

"Why can't we be friends now? . . . It's what I want.
It's what you want."

But the horses didn't want it—they swerved apart; the
earth didn't want it, sending up rocks through which
riders must pass single file; the temples, the tank, the jail,
the palace, the birds, the carrion, the Guest House . . .
they didn't want it, they said in their hundred voices,
"No, not yet," and the sky said, "No, not there."

A Passage to India,
E. M. Forster

1

To live in fear, they say,
is not to live at all. But it is
also not to die just yet.

Dustbrown, face streaked with
white, convulsively alert, the sparrow
who visits our rooftop birdhouse knows
a hunger wild as her fear.
Feathers barely soften the outline
of her armature—nerves wired
like a watchspring, shudder, blink, tick,
rupturing into flight even when nothing
threatens. She knows some eye is on her.

Such vigilance is equaled only by
the patience of one other, a perfect complement—
the patch of shadow blacker than the sootgrayed
tar, but dappled by two sunspots as twin geodes
of lightning-flecked rockcrystal might glimmer
from a mineshaft—the courtier, unruffled enemy
of this twitterclown's alarm. Oh murderous grace,
cat I have loved above all other cats, companion
of my desk and bed, tear-taster, anklet of fur
against November drafts, breath at my ear,

nip erotic at my knee, familiar of
my unremembered powers, he who bestows the rumble
of love at my first touch.

How commonplace, and how astonishing, I say,
that when the sparrow looks at all that
loveliness, she sees
a killer. He walks in beauty
like a death. Even when he sleeps
indoors, she fears him, head aswivel,
blood calling out to blood. Torn so
between, what good am I? Fool, madwoman,
hemophiliac of sentiment, I still imagine
a different way. He is such a special cat, I say,
so intelligent, so curious to learn,
decorous, gentle almost to a fault,
his survival without a keeper unassured.
Surely such a creature could make the leap
that closes not fang and gum on wingtip
but spans the mutation of self and other;
surely it is possible, surely
this one could do it, this one who
nibbles cheese and vegetables
with a cetacean smile, this one, surely.
How can he bear to manifest himself as death
to such an other?

He doesn't want to look like death, you say—
you who have sharpened long your claws
against the headwinds of what some call
nature to prove all things unnatural natural—
you, of all people, say, But it's his nature.
In fact, you say, he tries for camouflage
in his surroundings, to disguise himself so he
will look like anything but death to her. See
how pathetically he waits for her to comprehend
that really he is just a shadow, his hope
straining toward her trust?

And if *she* could make the leap, I agree,
not to erupt in flight and churn
the currents of her fear, but once, instead,
embrace her dive with full-arched wings
and glide through grace reckless as a leaf
of autumn lemniscates to meet the shade
cast by itself below; if once, I say,
in such abandon she could light, mad
as a saint, in blessing, on his head,
in proof of her imaginative power to conceive
he might be other than her death—

she'd die for it, you say. Something went wrong,
terribly wrong, on this planet, you say again.
I blink, and turn away.

2
July. Selected journal entries—and exits:

    Discarded in the gutter, a carton for a folding gate
    of wire and mesh, the kind you place at doorways and the heads
    of stairs: "Keeps Baby and Pets Contained but Happy," reads
    the text. Later, at sunset, the television mourns

    astonishing and commonplace news: a ten-year-old boy
    killed himself. His name was Santos.
    He had been depressed. He lived in the barrio
    and died there, hanging from his size-small belt in the shower,
    the one room where he could be alone a while
    without arousing envy.

    Our son is also ten, has his own room,
    weeps for a Santos he never met. He floats
    the currents of Satie's "Gymnopédies" amazing
    as an aerialist when practicing his music. He has
    a sparrow's nightmares, but he practices death, too,
    sometimes, in games. He is trying to not lie about that.

The street poster—a former comrade's blown-up
face proclaiming himself the last pure leader,
proclaiming himself betrayed by everyone, proclaiming
the catastrophes to come with joy so fearful
it smears the print: world famine and world war,
carnage, destruction, blood, apocalypse. "The hatred
that already burns in the hearts of millions is
going to spread and deepen," he exults, "so let's go
out and let's not only die—"
    —but let's live? I ask aloud—
"—but let's kill to make revolution."

This month, in this state, two thirteen-year-old
boys are standing trial for murder. At that age,
in the faith I left behind, they proclaim a boy a man.
Today, a new strong man outlawed all music
from his revolution, having already excluded women.

3
Not to simplify, not to, not to.
Women can also kill, can kill, can kill.
Forget me not   let me not   let me not fear.

The singsong twitter of the daft,
the lullaby of the long sleep,
the chant of a novice, the left-hand
sostenuto, the voluntary purr.
    I can do it I can do it I can do it.
The little brain that tried.

Can the mad sin?
No. They have cast their sin outside themselves
and that has made them mad.

Can the mad sin?
No. They are already damned.

Can the mad sin?
No. Sin requires choice.
Choice requires sanity.

Can the mad sin?
No. Both sanity and sin require choice.
They have chosen not to choose.

Can the mad sin?
No. It is (not) their nature.

Can the mad sin?
No. They have fallen into grace
on full-arched wings.

Can the mad sin?
Yes. I have fallen from grace, a leaf crisped
from the tree. I have fallen from grace
because the sin, which was my death, was beautiful.

4
I chose. I chose a different way. In proof
of lost imaginative powers, I did not choose
security, the sanitized brain, the heart content
with scraps from my cave-fire. I did not marry
Edgar Linton or even Tom Buchanan.
Heathcliff would be my husband, I would save
Gatsby for living greatness. I would make the leap
that was not in your nature or my own,
practicing not to die even at the price
of training the heart to love in fear,
a terror wild as hunger but as holy.
Surely I could do it. Surely
      —forget me not to simplify can kill—
you could. This time, on this planet even,
surely, yes, you said, hope straining toward my trust.

      Ding dong something wrong
      chime each season's chill
      time and treason will
      rhyme or reason kill

Can the mad sin?
Yes, oh yes:

For I myself have blinded both the doors
through which love might have entered
wearing any camouflage not yours.

5
Duel in the sun or the shadow,
it ends the same.
She rides on her revenge for days
to his desert hideaway. She fires
the signal shot. He shouts a welcome.
She aims at him, shoots, hits. He falls.
She screams his name and drops her weapons.
He struggles upright, aims, shoots her, and hits.
She falls. He screams her name.
How shocked each lover is to hit the mark aimed for.
How they crawl toward one another between
bullets, how they weep and curse and call
each other liars, how they bleed their parts
according to the rules.

I've heard your promises before, she rails.
How could you do this to me, he recites.
I'm dying, he calls, see, I'm a shadow now, come to me, hurry.
You lie, she sings, it's in your nature,
I was a fool. She claws the rockface, scaling
her own jagged hunger. Red lacy cuffs unfeather
from both her wrists. She climbs,
she reaches him, leaf dizzying upward in her
inner hurricane's blind eye.
"I love you," he sobs. At last and means it.
Kisses her and dies. One gesture
later—her hand poised on his head in blessing—
then she is dead as well.
High on their ledge above sunset and cliché
their bodies cling. Oh beauteous enemy.
Oh murderous grace, inevitable.

6

Until now, I'd have ended there. And been grateful.
(Transcendence, even "not at the last but
at the very last" still worth damnation.)
But this once I find myself
turn, imagining how to imagine
a way to descend and still live. This time,
am I done with deathbed reunions made possible
because only then we forgive one another
our individual means of survival?

Surely, this time, I am done with professions of love
between taking aim, surely done with
the beauty of sin, dying, death. Oh let me be
done with all revolutions that long for
catastrophe, done with this crawling
along the rockface, with training
my heart to live in love, killing for it,
coming undone.

Surely this time I will gather my wits, doggerel,
props, and exit this tragedy, knowing that some will say
this proves I lack tragic sense—but knowing the oldest
of tragediennes is always some terrified clown
circling a doom she insists is comedic,
and knowing as well how preposterous
I must look now, and how commonplace:
blind, bloody, convulsively alert, face streaked
with autumn, ridiculously
twittering I can do it rhyme and reason
I can do it, see?

Now, at the last, of course, something will
happen naturally not in our natures. It could be
anything except imagined until it appears—
only recognized then as then only inevitable.
Something to rupture even the best-trained heart

into dreading love possible: something all over
rock, beak, fang, right-hand melody,
something constraining again as a gate
meshed from nervewire—lost, dreamt, and familiar.

Then the eye burns as if it could see.
Then one of us says, Why can't we
love now? It's what I want. It's what you want.

But our shadows don't want it—they fade with the light;
the earth doesn't want it, sending up rocks
through which lovers must crawl single file;
the gutters, the roofs, the games, the asylums,
the leaves, the famished, the birdhouse . . . they
don't want it, they say in their hundred voices,
No, not yet, and the planet repeats, *No, not here*.

FIVE

THE HARROWING OF HEAVEN
A Passion in Seven Chakras

"The point of vision and desire is the same."
Wallace Stevens

I

The spine, that great question mark,
asks and asks how this can be, how
something can look through the eyes
of a mirror, or in at a window, to devastate
what had been real. It was given
up for lost; so much was against it—
all the world's suffering, all sense, craft,
intelligence, what we were trained to believe
was salvation and what, for the opposite reasons,
we came to believe was salvation, and the thin
thread of loving we persistently wind
around the spools and the rounds of our lives.
I had glimpsed it so often as to be sure
I imagined it: once, by candlelight
in the eyes of a boy who later hanged himself;
once in the laughter of a woman rising like steam
from a natural hot spring in the desert;
once in a dance my young son offered me;
more than once in touch or poems
of the man I lose and long for, living with daily;
but lineaments of gratified desire were most devised
by my mind's sorcery, to filter down diluted or brutalized,
although gratefully received, into the importing body.
A recluse in the towerbrain, no longer even bitter, I had
forgotten to pull up after me the frail bone ladder
that might sway in some unthinkable passion's storm,
or crack should anyone try to climb or should
I ever unlikely descend. So much was against it,

there, at the root, the foundation, where it would have
had to begin and could not be conceived.
    But it walks through the door, breathless
    from casual dawn devotions of running, sleep lying
    still like a milky ghost along eyelids and smile—
    and the voice like a knell tolling silently
    This can be. This can be. I exist.

2
The cells of the brain flare nova,
a starfall of still-burning shreds;

some energy is thinking through the body
more rapidly than mind can repair its synapses;

a rush of pure thought, somatic
meteorites raining across all intentions.

Everything is against it. Still, it has begun
irresistible to churn a current from bloodbrook

to bloodriver, thrumming each leg
kneeweak, both muscles and marrow

at the join of thigh to genitals
gone wax. Is this desire—this astonishment?

this glare of a star I know
for certain died long since?

This comes in shockwaves of silence
knocking me flat inside my own lungs,

skin flickering with the blood in revolt
just beneath, blood on the tongue, blood,

blood in the eye. More than desire
curiosity more than hunger or lust

curiosity famishes me,
this wanting to know, once, now, *now*,

whether it passed and I missed it,
whether it's been with me unrecognized,

whether it doesn't exist,
denies or describes my reality,

is fake or is holy.
Curiosity: that *is* desire.

3
We are stone creatures dancing
an intricate figure
of meaning that means other meaning;

each sentence, glance, gesture,
comes adorned with its own EXIT
sign, just in case.

Lust, we discuss, and danger, loneliness,
jealousy, madness, commitment, control—
my palms slick with fear, my lips parched.

Ridiculous, bland, unendurable,
we babble on about words
we think about thinking aloud

this cannot be desire *this can be*
"cathartic synergistic conceptual gestalt"
says one, "existential romanticism"

answers the other. This is inane and insane
—but something looks out of those eyes.
I exist, it proclaims, responding

directly in private discussion
to the blind tapping at the inner walls
of my belly, code lucid enough for whoever that is

in the neighboring cell.
Back and forth this interchange develops
while we pretend we express it

arguing cogently about cerebration, power,
what constitutes attraction, do I
want a beer, have you been in love

—and all the time love wears us
more and more tightly, growing into us
until the fit is so skinperfect

that when we think we move, love moves us,
and, moving, can afford
to let us say goodnight and think

we dance apart—as if we were not strung
on a thin thread already unwinding,
as if to let us go.

4
It's still too early in the year for roses,
yet what will be rose already swells along the branch
between thorns until it feels the furthermost edge
and can begin outfolding into space.

But the heart's wave over wave of pulsed budding
is late, lain in waiting, in readiness
gorged, knowing best its own blood, until each aortal
thorn glows iridescent, streaking a trail

of bleeding like a sign through the galaxy's flesh—
each a comet, an inflamed petal drifting clear

as the heartblossom slowly disrobes herself
guise by disguise, choice by choice risked:

—the unease of power at being the older,
—one card, the Page of Pentacles, turned up three times running,
—a careless permission from those who love in ignorance,
—cost prophecying madly in the temple, while through stamen,

stem, spine, root, soil, mattering energy sings *I exist*
and, like a dreamer waking her undreamt reality,
this woman worn by love, this body covering the heartbud
like a canvas sack against frost

makes her choices, goes about her preparations,
decides—eyes round with vintage terror
two decades old—to understand what she is doing,
to know, to choose, to enter into the layers

incarnadine of the heart's labyrinth,
daring for once intellect and compassion
to discover if lust can be so pure
that not crimson, no, nor scarlet, carmine, minium,

could rubify its immaculation
with love's untidyness, love's fullblown
blowsiness—so radical, awesome, slattern,
fanatic, fully armed, defenseless, and inevitable

that no heart's rose could pulse such pheremonic
perfume deliberately unplanned—
this risk worth taking as if there could be
any other choice but death.

5
Once, the Divine Obscene Dactyls were reverenced.
Pre-Mycenaean goddesses expose still bare hands
held up for adoring. Their breasts wear only

serpents, their eyes are round as The Five Holy Vowels
with watching inward through the Mystery, the maze

of bowel, bone, tendon, vein, dark drownings
down to the bloodsource then relentless up
again this time the current roaring toward
the arteries to crash in rapids against
wrist, ankle, temple, throat—heat

falling through the outermost edge of skin
to shower along the shimmering waves of air.
The entire torso, now, is heart and genitals;
no single part is localized but each
at once is every all where and the limbs

coiled for unfurling to a pentacle.
Oh parchment for words, oh page for pentacles,
hair dark, dark eyes fired in the broad-boned kiln
of your skull, how the night-sky has set to work
with materials so cheap as our brief flesh!

This pewter light, common as sculpt-metal,
builds itself upon our armatures, working
in to where love feels its way through darkness
by the thinnest thread unwinding, until we could
as well have been cast out of the purest silver.

Meanwhile we poise, two children on the meadowgrass
under bold stargleam, seducing each other
with talk, at the last, about art. Red wine, mosquitos,
lilac-oil electric at my wrists—and a sudden
stupefying arc shared by twin shooting stars.

So the long accelerating blur, as form
quickens to radiance, radiance moves across wet grass
and somehow into cabin, bed, arms lifted to praise,
lips, such nakedness—the panic snaps a tendril
green around my spine, but spirals lightward,

and blooms: burst throatflower of guiltless, shameless
utterance. I have never breathed this way before.
I am not breathing normally, not breathing, not,
I am breathing from a place deeper behind inside
my lungs and fear than I have ever let

be touched with oxygen. Syllables of laughter
float fragile, languid, up between such gasps.
Ease clarity delight simplicity
oh gradual sprung fountains, fingers, legs,
double-double-helix vinous, twining,

and the throat's parabola expressing
This can be I exist I choose I will
in capillaried counterpoint which sings
like lava firming but still warm as flesh rinsed
by a slow spring rain, sweet hiss of transformation.

One bird pours dawn out
beyond the window my god
birds will go on like
this tomorrow and it has
nothing to do with pain.

6
Whatever happens now—
whatever is pretended, argued, played,
betrayed, denied, admitted, noticed,
coarsened, discovered, ignored,
unsaid, or unforgotten—let there be
grief if necessary, but no regret.

It happened once at least utter
and perfect, a gift plain as clay or consonants
—a person, not an event,
who, even if misunderstanding it,
bore the full weight of the message.
It isn't necessary for the blessing to recognize itself.

Except that I want to whisper:
Be no longer afraid of the dark, my dear,
for you and I have been the dark,
have been the shadows by which love
too luminous to see directly etches its presence clear.
Your abstract concepts pale before such dark accomplishment,

such velour rays that the sun rose, smoking with sparks
struck from my eye that night, and later,
toward noon, when I lay tinder bellydown flat in tall grass
every blade I saw was edged in a discrete red-lilac
nimbus, erotic, tender, sacred, numinous even now
on each nerve's thin spooled filament still glowing.

You see, I think that long ago it passed
and I missed it; and also that it came to me
unrecognized; furthermore, that it doesn't exist,
describes and denies my reality, is fake
and is holy—and that never in my life
have I encountered something so familiar before.

I have been hated too long and skillfully by too many,
I have been loved too long and skillfully by one
—whose vision must have foreseen what all my labor
lost me—to deny you, imagine you, or fail
to remember each detail's precision I still can see
from which some cell of my sight will never look away.

7
The passion enters at the spine's taproot spiraling

       to exist

along the fuse of my own hooded serpent image, who blazes

       to desire

nourishes, shudders, sighs, in the cove of the belly

       to move

coiling toward its rosefire nest at the heart

       to choose

hands give it shape, throat gives it utterance,

       to will

transformed transenergy now visible, visible fleshly grace

       to see

how love triumphant scales and crowns the brain with art, all

       to create

       this

       poem.

THREE SALT SONNETS
TO AN INCIDENTAL LOVER

"They called Sophia salt. Without it, no offering is acceptable."
> The Gospel of Philip, II 3, from
> *The Gnostic Gospels of Nag Hammadi*

"Who will grieve for this woman? Does she not seem
too insignificant for our concern?
Yet in my heart I never will deny her,
who suffered death because she chose to turn."
> "Lot's Wife" by Anna Akhmatova
> (Kunitz and Hayward translation)

1

You were a man who could eat no salt, a trick
of your young blood, hardly your fault, heredity's
rush at too high pressure through arteries
stiff if cured by seasoning. All your lack
showed you not worth my salt—but sharper, mine
formed you the salt of the earth (though with a grain).
Have you heard that certain salts have a high melting point?
Some, when fused, can conduct an electric current.
Did you know that wars were fought for salt? I've learned
this stuff of life preserves. I lick each wound
we dealt me and taste the piquancy of your flight:
how, in vain thirst wild, you'll seek an antidote
bland enough to neutralize the flavors
of my skin's toxicity, my opiate tears.

2

I might have known such pungency as this
was common as salt, a chemical present in all
animal fluids. Not sure, I chose to bless
the thing with magical properties, to dwell

on its being one of the alchemist's three
primary elements: in contrast to sulphur
and mercury representing fixity—
although I didn't plan to stay forever.
I did develop a palate I don't regret
and will not sit below the salt, not ever
again. Now all I have to do is wait
or walk away—or live in savored fear
of looking backward, stricken, toward light's feast:
a pillar gesturing at the embers past.

3
The eye, perceiving shallows, looks beyond.
Farsighted, we stumble the Here; equally unsafe
myopic, we compensate by detail. Both distend
pleasure toward joy, discontent toward grief.
See how, one millimeter into marble,
the satyr's tragic socket stares past gimmick:
a common ploy of skill, desire, and chisel.
So were you deeper than you knew. Technique,
vision's sharp act, quarried you whole from my vein—
immortal, beautiful. Yet why, less artist than slave,
do I toil these mines which seem so un-Carraran
still, as if you could turn back to look alive?
This acrid element we carve is where we die.
The choice of medium is what blinds the eye.

THE UNDEAD:
A Pentacle of Seasons

I
In the spring the stranger
features of my lover's face seemed
puzzled now and then, his laughter
fading like the print of a kiss
as if he caught my glimpse of someone
alien in his face—your haunting,
your expressions poltergeisting
muscles of his eyelids, twitching his smile—
while I pronounced his name over and over
as exorcism, wondering all the while: *you,
is that you?*

2
In summer, someone claiming to be you
moved through our house each night
traversing all my distances with hate
as intimate and as effective as any tools
a torturer might wield to woo his prisoner
from silence. Not hate, you swore, but fear,
bitterness, anger, even hope—
yet what I fathomed under summer air
distorted by so many darkyears of expanding
space was hate. It felt like hate. It felt
as if hot music battered the walls with hate,
hate hissed from poems, hate shredded its own heat
like orange tongues spitting themselves out
on our hearth, hate whined and pounded its chest
naming itself love, hate clocked the hours
before dawn, tolling its rancid words
through what was once your voice. And I
kept silence, distance cool as pity
my one weapon, hardening, kept watch,

and thought: *that isn't you.*
Is that you?

3
With autumn came my flight
and her arrival—one woman borne
through the rising twilight chill,
leaf in the hurricane loosed from the tree,
the other russet-haired in drifts
of flesh settling above your body—
and I could see from all my distances
how, stranger, you rose up to meet her,
laughing, confident, young, your lips
the medium now of what had been my lover's
kisses, but for her. I saw, and murmured
through the shrinking light, "*Can that be you?*
Is that you?"

4
Cold such as this is unnameable,
winter a word of euphemism
for this lightless room at five
in the morning after the phone goes dead,
the last connection severed
by your fury reincarnate.
What grace I've conjured and now lost
leaves a perfume ghostly as dead flowers:
relics left from a withered miracle
are always only sentimental. Nothing is
feelable now but ice—at the foot, the brain,
the fingertips, the heart. Blind hands outstretched,
I glide my way to the mirror and touch
the frozen glass, my own outlines dim
in the leakage of windowed streetlight
as a traveler's shape seen far off
bending through a blizzard. *You,*
I would greet whoever that is

in the silver if my lips could thaw, *you,*
I would call to that self, *is that you?*

5
This will end, spring come again—and go—
wounds close despite their ritualized reopenings.
Justifications will be found, reasons
to explain why saints and lovers need
no longer walk the earth like fools.
It's no good pretending
that pretending isn't everything.
The healing power of mercy is relentless.

Lost lover, fallen saint,
more the fool I then, unasleep and dreamless,
to host the visitation two nights running
of myself:

> once in a gown and wimple, carrying
> book in one hand, basket of quince in the other,
> turning on the cobbles of a narrow street
> under the shadow-spire of a cathedral to confront
> the revenant of a man who follows me;

> and once in a tunic of silk disposable
> as paper, telecommuter in one hand,
> micro-computer library in the other,
> striding along a plaza bright in the three-moon
> marbled midnight, and stopping dead to encounter
> the holograph of a man before me;

and both times each time all times
seasonless echoing through the pretense
of time itself like sound distorted through space
calling out the pretense of recognition,
peering through darkness, squinting through light,
again and again barely whispering
to the stranger, *"You—
is that you?"*

DEPTH PERCEPTION

1

Desire is nothing
but the desire to break
the surface of all surfaces:

to speak one language without
articles or gender, past or future
tense, and pronoun-pure;

to understand at last the only
reason death is frightful—because
the corpse is wholly surface.

4

She was often all women. That was easy.
Could she still do this, faced with three actual women?
This was admittedly more difficult, but became
her—and was instantly comfortable
once she entertained the thought,

thinking it entertainment: this was to be a mere three women,
the other woman who slept with her Husband,
the other woman who slept with her Lover,
and herself—the Wife.

No. This was (remember) to be
fair: the woman who *loved*
the Husband, the woman who *loved*
the Lover, and herself—who loved as well

herself, only recently, fiercely, glory
and wonder, throat bared for laughing at last—
wait. This was to be (remember?) about all three,
this was to be instantly comfortable

once imagined. (Try again.) To enter deeply into
the woman who sits absently combing out her waist-length
hair, sable as no mermaid's but as sleek,
on a high floor by lamplight in a modern

city, while my Lover watches
slowly inhaling, thinking of the sculpture
he will build beached lonely in the southwest
desert, and her children quarrel in the next room.

Not so deeply in as to lose the possibility
of counterpoint. To enter also into the woman
who paces the small stone hut that is her
temporary study in an ancient city, circling

her typewriter like a target or the center
of a whirlpool which will drag her in
not to write her book's next chapter but
a letter of carefully understated longing

to my Husband—the tone desperately undesperate
but leaking the passion nonetheless that fists
her hands in the pockets of her caftan. Squared
in the window, the sunset irrigates the city's

terraces, each roof a rose fullblown in afternoon
light struck from the desert. I claim to understand
that she would walk with him there, strolling
the dusk bazaars, to loll at cushioned coffees—

just as I claim to understand that the other
would walk with the other in the other desert
around and around the circular sculpture he plans:
a flat, massive message to be seen from the stars.

Hubris to think the stars care, hubris
to think I know what either other would do.
For contrast, I make her hair red, or blonde, a cap
of wiry strands each one of which I invent entire.

Protection against precise detail, gratuitous hurt,
invasion of the privacy of pain, a libel suit
lodged in the court of the heart? Or lodged
in the throat, a stuck metaphor, a silence?

And why should both women be Jews? All three,
for that matter? It complicates things
even further in its irrelevance. No, dearest
self, it isn't that simple to break

the surface of three women.

7
The gesture is where philosophy enters poetry.
One window alight in a deserted building
at three a.m., the child's shrug, a dream.

Easy to break the Lover's surface, considering
I invented his depths. Yet have I ever
driven at night and driven, alone, insects

shocked into dead matter on the windshield's surface,
the injured car radio crackling Vivaldi and gospel
in alternate statics? Driving and driven in cloverleaf

circles, the yellow road-divider stuttering an infinity
of placelessness; afraid to go home. The matter
seeks the maker. There, look! This is the thing itself—

paper or wood from the same tree's assassination,
ink or paint, something by which to stain
the surface bright with images. And the thing is huge,

extraterrestrial, enormous—the structure, the poem,
vastly imperfect audacious rising
in celebration of not one single reason

but materials and vision, the act of conjuring
itself. As if a road-divider blurred into one ribbon
of light and then ceased, at the end of a charted road.

3
Is it possible to break the surface
of the Husband? Danger here unto death.
First, he can speak for himself.
Second, he has spoken for himself.
Third, he will speak for himself.

> (Would he like the Wife to be *able* to speak for him
> —to understand—but not actually to do so?)

First, the Wife tells him
that she has already been there, beneath his surfaces.
Second, she tells herself that
she has tried to be there for so long
and hard she stopped imagining where
she might be under her own (surface).
Third, she believes she has never
been able to enter.

> (Would she not rather think herself incapable
> of entrance than believe that he successfully
> denied her entry?)

A failure of imagination
that cannot imagine deeper than its old
or newest imaginings. This also would require
imagining how he can possibly imagine her,
as he (imagines he) claims to do.

Once, in a dream, the Wife saw the Husband
totally: he was ageless and naked, all power and grace,
beams of light streaming from the socket just above
his pelvic bone—light behind him, light,
light all around him, a rush of light like wind.

He offered her a comb, a gift for her hair, then
gold, later brown, now silvering.
It is possible that she never saw him again.

His depth resurfaces on his own page.

9
To ventriloquate oneself alone in the desert,
pure thought more real than merely being there:

pure desolate desert, the pin-pricked curve
of shadow overhead mocking with clues of luminescence
from some other universe but here rasping a wind
in dry heaves of inhumanity; the silence of whose
ego broken only by blood insistent in the ear,
breath unbidden in the throat; the sound of a first
footstep, unable to be still.

The act is where desire enters reality
or the reverse. The act stitches itself across them
like a dolphin breaking the surface between water
and horizon before it disappears from having been imagined.
Or do neither reality nor desire exist—
all acts as passionless as
they are unreal?

2
Is it self-congratulatory guilt
to imagine (at least on the surface)
that all of this is really the Wife's fault?

Proposition: If the Wife had remained
faithful after twenty years, there would
have been no Lover. If the Wife had not had
a Husband, the Lover might not have found
a different Woman. If the Wife had not had
a Lover, the Husband might not have sought

another Woman. The point of the surface
is to conceal. Under the surface

are wrists scarred with a palette-knife,
tangled bedsheets, the phone ringing at dawn,
the airport waitingroom in Vienna, cut flowers,
gallery catalogues, revisions of poems, revisions
of conversations, the fragrance of lilac-oil,
a crystal ball, a house of Tarot cards blown down,
chaos, the clay mask with no mouth.
These are sub-texts.

The point of the sub-text is to be heard
through the surface. What is not listened to
hardens into surface. Listen to it—and it becomes
the surface. What is concealed is never stationary. There
is always a new and newer surface. There is always something
under it, hot silver running under glass,
tomorrow's reflection, yet unimagined.

6
When she was twenty, the Wife wrote of her Husband
(not yet her Husband):

> A bull in the china-shops of the world,
> he functions cannily enough. Yet something
> seems to bulge just beneath his forehead
> and, after he's written a poem or made love,
> appears almost about to break the surface:
> a quality of rest, of radiance, which brings
> to mind all helplessly the word 'incarnate.'

When she was almost forty, the Wife
wrote of her Lover:

> This body: as if the bones of some internal storm
> had hurled the flesh up in such gentle swirls
> and dunes along the belly. These eyes

surprise sometimes even the rest of his face—
perhaps because looking at something
never seen before?

In between, whole lexicologies of sub-text,
dead languages, living tongues, whisper and hint,
hiss, sibilate, stammer, and sing

    springtime hearth-fires, the salt sand of the ocean
    (not the desert), faces changing at daybreak
    from Vikings into fauns, contents pages and corrected
    proofs, grocery lists, waiting and out-waiting, the birth
    of a child, shared anger at injustice, snow-angels
    in a deserted park, love voiced and fear unnamed,
    the presence of an unspeakable god.

You too, you handle memories like this,
again and again to recapture
their immediacy, until their shape is changed
by the handling—the over-read notated pages
difficult to scan for an original text—
and then at last the memories retain only
faintly their content, recording most sharply
the quality, substance, and form
of their handling.

5
There it is, like a bubble shocking glassiness
into ripples, like a mouth cut across skin
smooth with dead cells: they are all mothers,
all three women. A connection so simple

as to disgust. It, too, complicates matters,
but is even more relevant than having had Nazis
in common once. Are you lost?
So were all three women in, say, the fourteenth hour
of labor, hair so tarnished with sweat no one could tell
color or length, mouth dry as Death Valley,

something sub-alive battering toward reality,
the only entry through our flesh itself, we the surface

for someone else, wanting not to be,
feeling the surface of self torn open . . .
The Wife did not anticipate this particular
connection. She had perceived certain others:

the way the Husband's Woman feels on reading
a love poem he has written to her,
the way the Lover's Woman feels when he
carries her to bed. Admittedly, even these

seemed simple, like circumscribed grief.
Yet these, in fact, already lay beneath further
layers of still more simplistic empathy:
the ones declaiming that all men were cruel,

or fools, or little boys, or at least grossly
imperceptive—or even alike. This new fact
that bubbled up, however, was once heard
undeniable, humiliating, ecstatic, unconnected

at the prehistoric depth to Husband or Lover,
organic piece with desert, stars, something enormous,
mocking, extraterrestrial, audacious.

In the space of this writing,
it has healed bland as freshly silvered glass.

8
The impure act is the only act
possible, its placenta as luminous
as the shards of a mirror. It is the distant
sign, unreadable, the cry in an unknown language
lodged in the throat or the phone wire.
Suppressed, it is murderous; expressed, meaningless.

(Try again. Remember.)

Words die along the air, like light.
I, who once wrote this, was not three women,
not even one. I was not Mother, Jew, Lover,
or Wife. I was

a consciousness imagining
a reader who imagined this poem.

These are not words on a page.

THE HALLOWING OF HELL
A Psalm in Nine Circles

"Why, this is hell, nor are we out of it."
Marlowe's *Doctor Faustus*

1

The Rider is stationary
in Einstein's democratic universe;
all objects rush past her.
What rushes toward
wears bluish light: high frequency and energy.
What rushes away
wears reddish light: low frequency, low energy.
We each observe the same
laws of physics, but every individual
view is relative, despite all mass and all energy
being in fact equivalent.
Material falling toward a Black Hole would liberate
tremendous energy just before vanishing into it.
Black Holes, in turn, release enormous energy
by swallowing stars.
"All of astrophysics," the scientist says,
"is about nature's attempt to free the energy in matter."
The impossible must happen.
The Rider moves.

(*Stay in motion.*)

2

You have gained the Self.
Sunset slanting through a glass of burgundy,
a sparrow wading in the fountain,
a dead man on the phonograph singing
a lullaby to his son.
A dead woman's villanelle

about practicing loss.
Your mother's hands, attached
to your wrists now, lying in your lap;
your son's hands, in a distant room,
practicing the Bach "Solfegietto" you played
long ago. Enemies insisting god exists
and friends proclaiming there's no god.
You are losing the Mother,
you may yet lose the Husband,
you have lost the Sister,
you will lose the Child,
all in the nature of things.
But you have gained the Self.

Everything *seems*. The sun,
for example, is a globe of burgundy glass.
What profiteth it you
to lose the whole world if
you gain your own soul?

(*Try, at least try.*)

3
Let us say
she is still unfashionably metaphysical,
hopelessly so, unsalvageable, damned.
Let us admit that she has abused
this dubious gift, herself, on occasion—
not only cynically to deny it, but
worse: to use it as escape, abstraction,
ectoplasm to wisp away the sacred Specific
(though not the political). Now
she still tries all broken bitter to bless
each thing with magical properties,
to see mystery where no mystery exists,
embarrassing good people who believe
that once you look deeply enough
into the eyes of suffering you
can see nothing else again.

Life have mercy upon us.
Death have mercy upon us.
Life have mercy upon us.

Let us try.

(Start with whatever your glance first falls on.)

4
The flowers on my desk
are lilies: lemon lilies,
Peruvian lilies, and *gloriosa.*
Praise be to real things, simple, lowly,
praise be the words to name them.
Praise be to Phosphor, our larkspur Siamese,
in her circle of sleep under the desk lamp.
Praise be to paper and ink, pencil and typewriter.
Praise be to the city beyond my window, stirring
into dawn, praise to the lemonlily-colored
orange juice in my glazed pottery cup,
the books ranged like armies of unalterable light
along my shelves; praise be to those, alive or dead,
who wrote them, those who published them,
who printed, bound, sold, bought them,
who gave them to others, and who read them.
Blessed be the existence of the possibility of
poetry. Blessed be the flowers on my desk.

(A beginning. Now. Again.)

5
And blessed be the women who get you through:
the woman who lets you stay in her apartment,
the woman who takes you out for a drink,
the woman who guides you through the House of Mirrors
    in Copenhagen's Tivoli,

the woman who walks you through the Belvedere
    gardens of maroon-stalked orange gladioli,
the woman who loans you money,
the woman who has fresh Kleenex,
the woman who offers to chart your horoscope,
the woman who writes a stranger a letter about her poems,
the woman who sells your jewelry for you,
the woman who feeds your cats when you're gone,
the woman who makes you laugh,
the woman who tempts you to a superficial movie,
the woman who sees through Aquinas,
the woman who gives you a ream of 20-pound bond paper,
the woman who always seems to have an extra concert ticket,
the woman who prays for you,
the woman who writes her own books,
the woman who insists you keep a set of her keys,
the woman who gets you a poetry reading,
the woman who rings up to see how it's going,
the woman who loans you a book,
the woman who loves a man and is going through the same thing,
the woman who loves a woman and is going through the same thing,
the woman who gives you an inflatable travel pillow,
the woman you can show a first draft to,
the woman who cries with you,
the woman who makes you eat something,
the woman who gives you work to do,
the woman who reminds you to be fair,
the woman who helps you face answering letters,
the woman who talks about light,
the woman who falls in love with you
    but remains your friend,
the woman you yourself once loved above all women—
    weaned before her time, who hates you for that
    weaning now—blessed be her freeing vengeance even;
blessed be all the love like waves of light
    of all the others.
Blessed, blessed be the women who get you through.

      (Good. Again now, again.)

6

To build a heaven in hell's despite
is not so necessary, given such a world.
Once, snorkeling in Paraíso Reef off Mexico,
we entered an innocent universe, if not
a democratic one. Black coral,
fiery feather stars, and sea lilies waltzed
with the current, and the fish called
Shy Squirrels played between our outstretched fingers.
A Queen Angelfish, all prismiridescent,
made her fastidious progress past spiny sea urchins.
The only sound was my own breathing—and a Yellow Grunt
sucking calmly on algae, the only light
that which refracted through water in patterns duned
like stretchmarks on a pregnant woman's belly,
a splendor of design. That light rushed
neither toward you nor away from you; it swayed
around you, bathed you, it became the water.
I swam through it, weightless as a swallowed star
moves, moving, moved. In such a world,
the task is less to build
than excavate a heaven in hell's despair.

(*Better and better. Now, again.*)

7

So blessed be the child you call your son;
may his paths be lit with grace.
Blessed be his understanding,
the wisdom he almost knows he already has.
Blessed be his piano keys and clarinet keys
and lost skatekeys and doorkeys.
Blessed be his grief for battered children
and for baby seals and the great whales, blessed
his love of Shakespeare and snowballs.
Blessed be his magic spells and home runs,
his dungeons, his dragons, his Debussy, his dolls,
blessed be his wit's edge and his compassionate heart,

blessed be his friends and phone calls and the first
leaves of his sexual budding.
Blessed be his sense of justice, his anger
and defense of his own rights.
Blessed be his rebellion against you.
Blessed be the boy you call your son.

(*Here it is. Try. Again. Again.*)

8
And blessed be the man I've lived with almost twenty years.
Blessed be this past year of unspontaneous combustion.
Blessed be our two dead selves who died that year;
may they rest in peace.
Blessed be the dogged, furious, insistent
capability of change.
Blessed be his eyes, dark never except with pain,
but mostly the color of sunlight glimpsed looking up
from under the sea surface—a bluish light,
high frequency, that rushes toward you.
Blessed be his just anger, blessed
all his lightbulbs changed and garbage taken out,
his mislaid eyeglasses and lost wallets,
blessed be the blood-jet of *his* poetry,
blessed be the friends who get him through,
blessed be his scratched Keith Jarrett and Scriabin records,
blessed be his fuchsia flowers and his precious
jacaranda tree, blessed be
the kiss we shared in an open field, thunderstorm-soaked
among the ruins of Mayan sacrifice.
Blessed be the sight of him underwater, each
of us beckoning, watching through respective masks
and smiling above teeth clenched around our oxygen.
Blessed be his fear of the living god
in himself, and his love of that. Blessed
be his face, laughing, between my laughing knees
one August afternoon, blessed be
all the moments-into-years with him—

including the terror, the despair, the mutual
cruelties and cowardices.
Blessed be the years to come, together or apart,
for something in each of us is eternally
equivalent, matter and energy, to something
in the other. Blessed be his courage and his genius,
his Tarot deck and Buddhist beads, his love
of men and his disowning masculinity.
Blessed be life with him and without him,
blessed be the utterly new questions broken open now
and blessed be the lack of tidy answers.
Blessed be the man I'll love in some way till I die.

(Yes yes again yes again again yes)

9
Blessed be the hands that dare write this.
Blessed be even my failures, hypocrisies, self-
sustained martyrdoms—blessed be their recognition.
Blessed be the child I was; I gather her
and all her discrete pain into my arms.
Blessed be the crochety, eccentric, and terrific
raucous wise old woman I intend to be; I gather
her decaying matter into my arms.
Blessed be all my fears and the losing of them,
all my loves and the losing of them,
all my lives and the losing of them;
blessed be the rose light they recede in.
Blessed be whatever comes, floating
in a luminescence blue and inevitable as the sea.
Blessed be this continual unrelenting constant gradual
hallowing of hell, of everything I know
and everything I meet for the first time,
this great work of living.
Blessed be the energy of dark stars and the light
of long-dead suns, the ongoing task
to see as holy, to make holy
every specific particle one can imagine, the imagination

holy. Blessed be the heights and the depths.
Blessed be change—and its sense of humor.
Blessed be survival—and its sense of honor.
Blessed be death—and its sense of relief.
Blessed be life—and its sense.
Blessed be the eyes that dare read this.

>Hosanna in the highest
>Hosanna in the lowest
>
>As it was never before,
>is not now and yet shall be,
>worlds without end
>
>*Again*

Of Robin Morgan's previous books of poetry, *Monster* and *Lady of the Beasts,* a review in *Poetry* (Chicago) declared: "Robin Morgan will soon be regarded as one of our first-ranking poets." These collections were especially welcomed by women for the passion with which they articulated feminist consciousness. Morgan also compiled and edited the now-classic anthology *Sisterhood Is Powerful,* and authored *Going Too Far: The Personal Chronicle of a Feminist,* a collection of her essays from the 1960's and 1970's. She was awarded a National Endowment for the Arts Literature Grant in Poetry, and her poems have been published widely in both literary and political journals, and have been translated into French, German, Arabic, Turkish, Russian, and Japanese. A Contributing Editor to *Ms.* Magazine since 1976, she is a recipient of the Front Page Award for Distinguished Journalism. She lives in New York City with her husband, the poet Kenneth Pitchford, and their son, Blake Ariel. She is currently at work on a new prose book, *The Anatomy of Freedom,* and on a fourth collection of poems, and has begun compiling and editing *Sisterhood is Global: The First Anthology from the International Women's Movement.*